GOLDBERG
BAIL BONDS

Municipal Monument

A Centennial History of the Municipal Building
Serving Minneapolis and Hennepin County, Minnesota

by

Paul Clifford Larson

Municipal Building Commission • Minneapolis • 1991

On the cover: The center panel of the triptych window in the rotunda of the Municipal Building. Frontispiece: The Municipal Building, Minneapolis, 1990. The decorative page border throughout this book is adapted from the plaster dado in the Fifth Street vestibule. The initial cap design at the beginning of chapters is from the iron baluster of the staircase.

Illustration credits: Cover photo by Gerald Gustafson; frontispiece and pp. 50, 67, 70, 79, 103, photos by George Heinrich; p. vi, courtesy of Municipal Building Commission; pp. vii, 101 (*Popular Mechanics*), courtesy of the Office of the Hennepin County Sheriff; pp. 2, 41, 42 top, 96, 97 (WPA), 98 (WPA), *Minneapolis Journal* photos courtesy of Minnesota Historical Society (MHS); pp. 4, 9, 64-66, 71, 91, photos by Paul Clifford Larson; pp. 5, 32, 33, 37, 88, from Isaac Atwater, *History of the City of Minneapolis* (New York: Munsell and Co., 1893); pp. 6, 13, 39, 84, courtesy of Minneapolis Public Library (MPL); p. 7, from *Minneapolis Through a Camera* (Minneapolis: Board of Trade, 1896); p. 8 left *(1885 Hopkins Atlas)*, 8 right *(1892 Foote Atlas)* Minneapolis History Collection, courtesy of MPL; pp. 10, 20, 42 bottom, 52, 53, 62 bottom, 76, 80, 82, 85, 87, 90, 93, 94, courtesy of MHS; p. 11, Illingworth photo, Bromley Collection, courtesy of MHS; pp. 12, 21 top, 23, 77 right, 83, 86, courtesy of Hennepin County Historical Society (HCHS); p. 14 from Mariana Briswold Van Rensselaer, *Henry Hobson Richardson and his Works* (New York: Dover Publications, 1969); pp. 16, 17, 44, 49 bottom, 59, 75, Sweet photos from *A History of the Municipal Building* (Minneapolis: Board of Court House and City Hall Commissioners, 1910); p. 19, courtesy of Northwest Architectural Archives, University of Minnesota; pp. 21 bottom, 22, 23 bottom, 24, from *Supplement to Northwestern Architect,* April 1888; p. 25 from *American Architect and Building News,* April 7, 1883; p. 26, from *Supplement to Northwestern Architect,* August 1888; p. 27, from *Minneapolis Spectator,* courtesy of HCHS; p. 30, courtesy of Department of Housing Inspection, City of Minneapolis; p. 31, from Alfred Söderströns, *Minneapolis Minnen* (Minneapolis: privately published, 1899); p. 34, from *Men of Minnesota* (St. Paul: R. L. Polk and Co., 1915); p. 35, from *Northwestern Architect,* courtesy of MPL; p. 36, from *Minneapolis Sunday Tribune,* Nov. 10, 1895; p. 39, from Bromley Collection, courtesy of HCHS; pp. 40, 78, Sweet photos, courtesy of MPL; p. 42 left from *Minneapolis Tribune,* Nov. 23, 1895; pp. 43, 44 top, 46, 60, Sweet photos courtesy of MHS; p. 45, from *Minneapolis Journal,* Nov. 11, 1895; p. 47, from Long and Kees sketches (Series K, Book 9), Municipal Reference Library; p. 48, from *Minneapolis Journal,* Aug. 17, 1895; p. 54, from W. H. Hazen, *The City of Minneapolis* (Minneapolis: privately printed, 1891); p. 55, from reduced copy of 1888-1889 working drawings, Municipal Reference Library; p. 56, courtesy of Floyd Scott, via Hennepin County Public Affairs Office; pp. 57, 61 top, 62 top, from Horace B. Hudson, ed., *A Half Centry of Minneapolis* (Minneapolis: Hudson Publishing Co. 1908); pp. 28, 58, 69, 74, from Long and Kees office brochure, Minneapolis, 1896; p. 68, from Winslow Bros. brochure, 1892, courtesy of Chicago Landmarks Commission; p. 72, from *Minneapolis Sunday Journal Tribune,* Nov. 5, 1950; p. 81, Hibbard Studio photo courtesy of MPL; p. 95 top (March 10, 1939), 95 bottom (Feb. 23, 1936), 99 (Nov. 18, 1949), courtesy of MPL; p. 97 top, from *Minneapolis Times-Tribune,* Dec. 15, 1939, courtesy of MPL; p. 100, *Minneapolis Star-Journal* photo courtesy of MHS.

Editing, design, production: E. B. Green
Indexing: Suzanna Moody
Printing: Cooperative Printing
Manufactured in the United States of America

© 1991 by Municipal Building Commission. All rights reserved.
Library of Congress Catalog Card Number: 91-62011
ISBN 0-9630086-0-9

10 9 8 7 6 5 4 3 2 1

Contents

Foreword

Even in a wonderful and vibrant downtown with many spectacular buildings, the Municipal Building is special—not only because of its beauty but also because it is a key link to our past.

Planning for the Municipal Building started in the late 1880s when Minneapolis was in the midst of its greatest boom. It was a time to think big—who knew what the city might become?—and civic leaders boldly planned a structure that could serve as the seat of government for a much larger community. They also insisted that the new edifice be beautiful and monumental. The result was the Romanesque Revival building that is cherished so much today by citizens of Minneapolis and Hennepin County.

This book, written to commemorate the hundredth anniversary of the laying of the cornerstone, tells the story of the Municipal Building. We think citizens who read it will develop an even greater appreciation for the wonderful building we have inherited. And we suspect they will not be satisfied when they finish. With appetites whetted, they will want to examine the Municipal Building themselves, discover anew its beauty, and perhaps learn of some of its surprises and secrets.

—The Members of the 1991 Municipal Building Commission

—John E. Derus, Chair
Hennepin County
Board of Commissioners

—Donald M. Fraser
Mayor
City of Minneapolis

—Judy Makowske
Hennepin County
Board of Commissioners

—Alice W. Rainville
Minneapolis
City Council

Preface

For over thirty-one years, because of my service first as an assistant county attorney and then as Hennepin County sheriff, I have called the Minneapolis Municipal Building my second home. One cannot possibly spend so much time in one place without forming some opinions about it. I have come to think of my workplace as both delightful and impressive, both friendly and grand.

My interest in the Municipal Building first became manifest about six years ago when I began research on details of the only hanging carried out in the Municipal Building's county jail, in response to frequent questions from members of the public. Vivid newspaper accounts of the 1898 hanging indirectly provided new insights to the building, particularly the physical arrangements of the jail. The character of the building in general soon captured my attention.

About the same time, Roy N. Thorshov, of the architectural firm of Long and Thorshov, presented me with a 1910 mint-condition copy of an early (1887-1909) history of the building. He had received this book from his father, Olaf Thorshov, a member of the architectural firm of Long, Lamoreaux and Long, predecessor to his son's firm and successor to Long and Kees. The latter firm was the one selected in 1888 to design a new government building for the City of Minneapolis and Hennepin County. The 1910 book served as a springboard for my subsequent research and eventually to the commission of this book.

My studies have left me in awe not only of the building's grandeur but also of the architects who created a monument that will demand public respect and gratitude for years to come. Hardly a day passes that my travels in and out do not yield a new-found detail tucked away in a corner of the rotunda, gazing down from an entryway arch, or suddenly illuminated by the sun. Mischievous grotesques, radiant stained glass, grand marblework, and a host of other treasures await all careful observers.

Originally intended to last only 50 years, the Municipal Building, whose cornerstone was laid a century ago, now serves as a hub for the Hennepin County Government Center (completed in 1975)to its immediate south and the soon-to-be-completed federal courthouse on the north. While its Richardsonian style of architecture has given way to the brick, steel, and glass of the newer constructions, the Municipal Building provides a historic counterpart, a setting for the new that reminds us of where we have come from. Despite a host of structural changes since 1910, the Municipal Building retains its welcome, dignity, and grace. Thus historians, architects, and citizen admirers will, I am convinced, continue to resist any effort to permit this marvelous work of art to become anything less.

I hope that as you begin to turn the pages of *Municipal Monument,* you, too, will come to better know and to fall in love with the building that captured my heart years ago.

—Don Omodt
Hennepin County Sheriff
Honorary Chair
Centennial Commemoration Committee
Minneapolis

Acknowledgments

This book has two muses. One spoke to the author, who in 1988 produced an architectural exhibit for the University of Minnesota Art Museum. The Municipal Building figured heavily in that exhibit, and I was casting about for ways to keep the importance of that monument alive to the area after the show was off to other places. The other muse spoke to Hennepin County Sheriff Don Omodt, who loved the Municipal Building as no one else, who knew the cornerstone centennial was approaching, and who was looking for ways to bring it to life. When the muses met, the idea of this book was born.

Bringing the idea to fruition could not have happened without the support of the Hennepin County and City of Minneapolis governments at several levels. The Municipal Building Commission, which has kept the building alive and well over the years, generously funded all phases of book production, providing useful guidance at the outset but otherwise leaving the author a free hand. The Municipal Reference Library, housed in that still-miraculous stack of galleries within the tower, bent its rules toward a hands-on search for hidden resources. The Office of the Sheriff, the seat of the building's greatest enthusiast, provided use of a word processor to copy manuscripts as well as space for meetings and research.

Newspaper research was incalculably shortened by David Erpestad's monumental survey of *Minneapolis Journal* references to the Municipal Building, compiled in 1982 and 1983 while he studied under the architect of the building's restoration plan, Foster Dunwiddie. Another unpublished document, "The Historic and Architectural Significance of the Municipal Building, Minneapolis Minnesota" by Steven Ristuben and William Scott, contains a list of all surviving working drawings of the Municipal Building as well as the germ of the chronology in this volume. The City Hall and Courthouse Committee, a mixed group of Minneapolis officials and citizens, was behind both those papers, the first by way of suggestion and the second by direct sponsorship. By bringing the architectural significance of the building back to public consciousness, the committee was an indirect sponsor of this essay.

Three individuals deserve special thanks. Nancy Grell of the Municipal Building Commission choreographed an array of meetings and decision-making processes to get the project under way. She never wavered in her enthusiastic support of the book, even when I moved out of the state, got married, and had a child in the course of writing the manuscript. My friend and associate Charles Devol Test, a patriot of historic Minneapolis, tirelessly processed pages of minutes from meetings of the Board of Court House and City Hall Commissioners and remained on call for research assistance. Finally, my editor, Ellen Green, has had to work with deadlines made nearly impossible by the delay of the manuscript. To her flexibility, ear for the proper tone and pitch, and tenacity throughout production, this book owes its completed form.

To my patient wife, Pamela, and newborn son, Griffin, I owe the largest debt of gratitude, and with it a promise of the day when, book in hand, they can see the building for themselves and know it was worth it all.

—Paul Clifford Larson

Gardner Museum of Architecture and Design

Quincy, Illinois

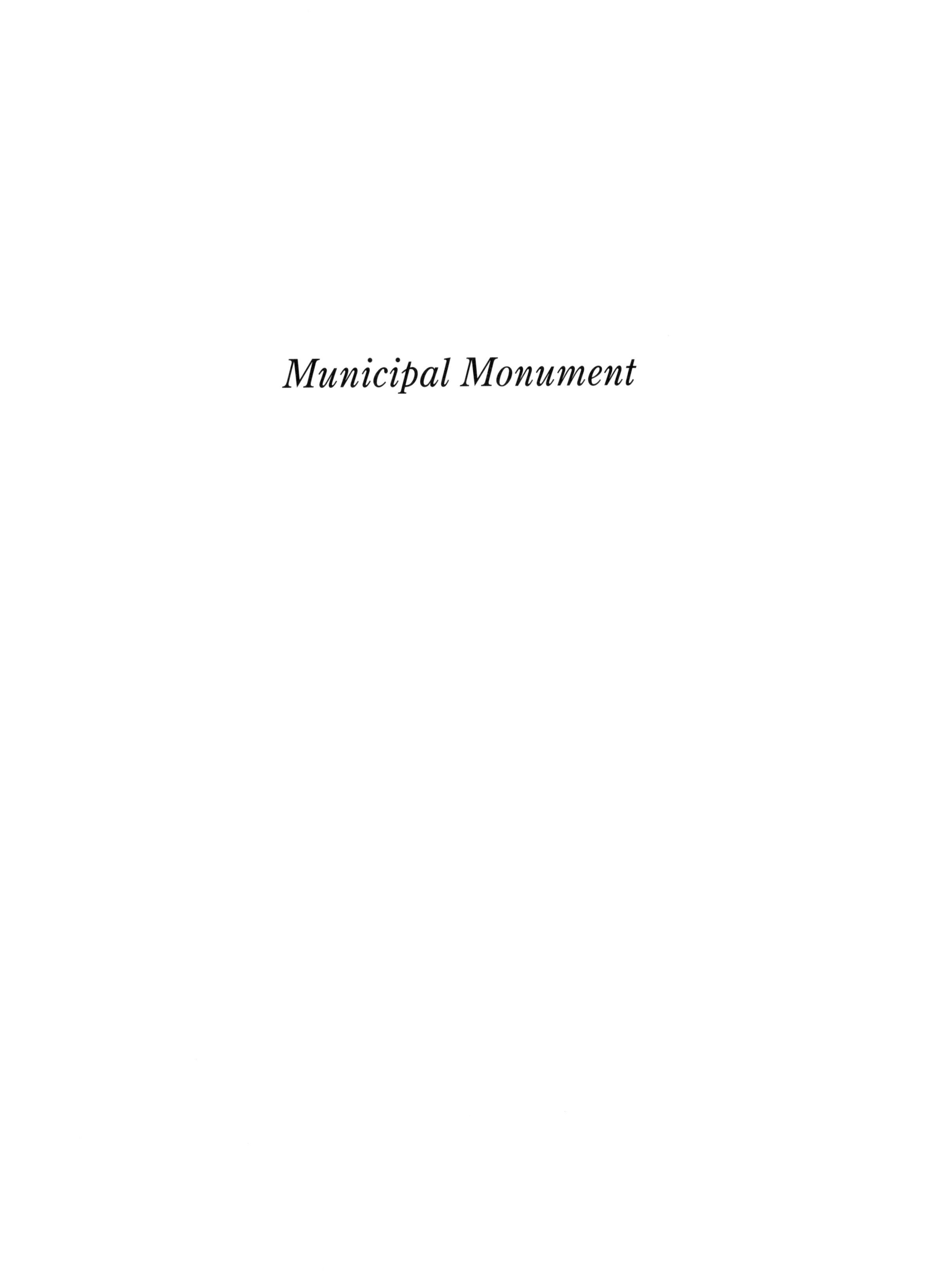

Municipal Monument

The reality of the Municipal Building, shown in 1903, rose to the vision of its planners. One newspaper reporter noted: "Its imposing elevation, and its magnificent proportions, covering as it does an entire square, would do credit to the largest city in the land."

The Idea of a Municipal Building

In a democratic society, every important civic building wears two faces. One wears a welcoming smile addressed without regard to wealth or social position to the public that supports and uses the building. The other wears the solemn gaze of a monument aspiring to artistic significance and a piece of immortality.

Much of the early history of the Municipal Building in Minneapolis can be conceived as an attempt by city and county fathers to keep these two faces from staring each other down. From the outset, there was a consensus among the building's sponsors and planners that it be a primary symbol of shared political and social ideals. It was to testify to the growth and importance of Minneapolis and Hennepin County as communities, not to the power of their governments as such. And yet—here is the other face—it was also to be a monument and as such to occupy an elite place among the buildings of the city and state. Monuments bite off a piece of immortality, and immortality does not come cheap. So immediate social and economic considerations, and with them the express concerns of the laboring class, were not to rule the day uncontested.

The clashing roles of the building in public life were clearly expressed by the ambiguous stance of public officials and the media in regard to the cost of the building. On the one hand, members of the Board of Court House and City Hall Commissioners (hereafter Board of Commissioners) continuously went on record in favor of "building for the future" and "not skimping on materials." That meant, among other things, building with sandstone and granite rather than local limestone and brick, overbuilding the internal structure so that partition walls could be moved at will, and creating one story more than the governments could fill.

The object was a building that could serve three-quarters of a million people, roughly triple the population of the county when the project began. The materials and workmanship for the interior spaces were continuously upgraded, and the architects were retained to design or supervise the design of nearly all the fittings and furnishings. These are all features of the project in its monumental aspect, which looked to the future for vindication.

On the other hand, the most oft-repeated boast about the Municipal Building was how inexpensive it was compared to like buildings elsewhere in the country. The architects were hired in large part because their design was specifically responsive to the stipulated budget. As that budget crept steadily upward from $1.15 million to $1.5 million to $2 million and finally, by 1905, to $3.5 million, the increases were constantly defended as "cheap" for what the public was getting—a structure that cost half the going square-foot rate for public buildings.

The difficulty in reconciling immediate public interests with long-range objectives and aesthetic ideals produced years of conflict over the design and cost of the Municipal Building. The trick was to create a building for the citizenry at large while instilling values that outstripped immediate and practical needs. That meant getting the public to identify its interests with the city of the future and, to some extent, with the values of a social class with money to spare. As a writer for the *Minneapolis Tribune* put it later, the city and county "erected a building which posterity will pay for and which posterity therefore, if it were on earth, should have had a voice in its planning; as it is, the present generation are but the guardians of the people who will pay for this structure."

Details of the Municipal Building like this doorknob and plate would attest to the vision of a grand monument for the common people.

The Vision of a Municipal Building

Much of the language and content of the vision that helped create the Municipal Building seems foreign today. Being the tallest, largest, grandest, most beautiful, costliest, or most economical public building in the Midwest is of no particular distinction anymore. From today's more cosmopolitan perspective, these boosterist claims seem foolish. But boosterism was more than one-upmanship. Tied to the parochial boasts of nineteenth-century Minneapolitans were a deep sense of civic pride, a communal sense of well-being, and dreams of a future offering their children a richer culture than they were able to enjoy. All these kinds of pride attached to public buildings of the community.

The idea that a grand and costly building should serve the interests of common people, indeed should symbolize their equality with social and economic betters, is not a modern conception. The pilgrimage churches and cathedrals of western Europe served such an ideal, however imperfectly. Members of all classes of society entered by the same door and took communion at the same table, just as judge, councilperson, custodian, and disgruntled taxpayer walk the same halls of the great modern civic building. This analogy between ancient church and modern civic building may seem farfetched today, but it was utterly plausible in late-nineteenth-century America. Great civic buildings occupied the places within cities where in another time cathedrals might have stood. Churches still vied for the highest ground and competed for the tallest spires, but their dominance in the heart of the city yielded to the monuments of government and commerce.

The Municipal Building also captured, in a loose sort of way, popular perceptions of the ethnic roots of the city. As U.S. Senator (Minnesota, 1889-1895) William D. Washburn observed in 1890, "the native-born population of Minneapolis is exclusively of northern origin, with a large infusion of New England blood." When the building was officially opened in 1895, local papers linked it to both the New England meetinghouse and the earthen walls within which the Teutons held their councils. Its style was referred to as "Norman," the English name for the Romanesque style introduced from France during the Norman Conquest, despite the obvious French antecedents for the castlelike massing of the building and the architect's published references to the Italian character of the tower. The very crudity of the surfaces and simplicity of the form spoke of northern vigor and hardihood, as opposed to the soft Mediterranean airs of the competing Classical Revival styles.

U.S. Senator William D. Washburn

In a more down-to-earth vein, the use of a building style based on collaboration between ancient architectural arts such as stonecutting and ironmongery was also a clear outgrowth of the late-nineteenth-century reaction to the erosion of the human environment and loss of individual identity sponsored by the Industrial Revolution. The reaction began in England in what came to be called the Arts and Crafts movement. By the late 1870s, these ideas had taken a firm hold on the leading architectural practices of this country. In this context, the modern civic building became a showpiece of individual artistry as well as of up-to-date planning. The new, secularized "cathedral" brought together the diverse creations of hundreds of workers, each carrying the skills and products of his craft or trade organization. The list of artisans and workshops contracting with the Board of Commissioners, all acknowledged leaders in their trades, is evidence such a process was at work in Minneapolis.

The city had come a long way in ten years. Barely a decade before the Municipal Building was planned, the Minneapolis downtown was largely composed of quickly constructed frame buildings. By 1882, it boasted 224 buildings of stone and 347 of stone and brick, however crudely most were carried through. By 1886 Minneapolis was the fastest-growing city in the country. It had attracted a group of young, eastern-trained architects of great ability, and it was in the midst of converting its streetscapes into an imposing array of monuments. The Minneapolis Public Library, Masonic Temple, and Lumber Exchange were all under way and each one played imaginatively on the neo-Romanesque themes of famed Boston architect H. H. Richardson. The culmination of these themes, and of Richardson's influence in the city, was to be the Municipal Building.

The sponsoring of an open architectural competition expressed the desire of city and county officials to make a regional or even national mark. It was plain from the first that local architects would be given preference, but the widespread publication of the competition circular brought national attention to the city and the project. Even after the architects had been chosen and the plans twice revised, the Board of Commissioners devoted enormous energy to ensuring that the new Municipal Building would not simply be the best Minneapolis had to offer but the finest in the United States. As the *Minneapolis Journal* reported at the cornerstone laying, "Its imposing elevation, and its magnificent proportions, covering as it does an entire square, would do credit to the largest city in the land."

The Municipal Building was from the first conceived as a megablock in the full modern sense: an architecturally unified, multiple-use development to fill an entire city block. In the Minneapolis downtown of 1887, a project of that magnitude was not just unusual but unique. Even the much-praised Syndicate Block of 1883, though it spanned an entire block on one side, was terminated by a rear alley. The city had to wait for the Butler Warehouse of 1906 to see a downtown development matching the scale of the Municipal Building.

Only the Exposition Building of 1886 approached the size of the Municipal Building, and it was across the river, on the outskirts of downtown development. Curiously, the only nineteenth-century megablock developments in the Twin Cities apart from public buildings were major breweries, like the public buildings, vaguely medieval in form. But the breweries were castles of a different order, consciously and conspicuously eclectic, as if to suggest an evolution of several hundred years of Germanic history. The Municipal Building was instead all of one piece, a single overwhelming presence.

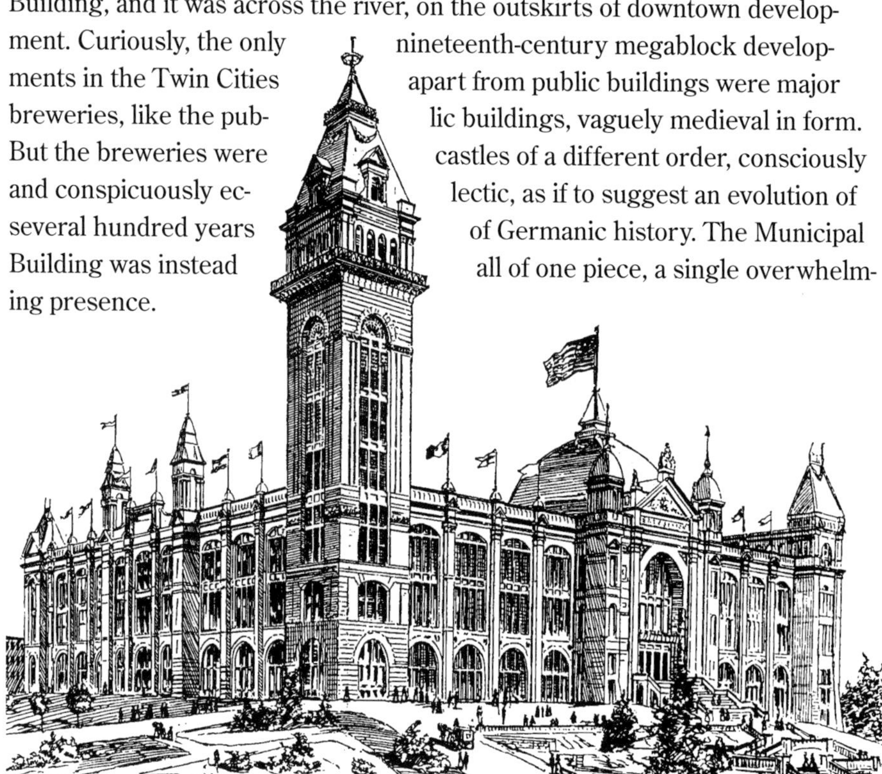

The Exposition Building of 1886 was the only structure in the city approaching the size of the Municipal Building. Built to the plans of Isaac Hodgson, it was 360 by 340 feet, the size of a city block from curb to curb.

The location of an 1880s megablock development several blocks from the downtown core anticipated a theme Minneapolitans have heard many times since. At the time the site was being determined and defended, the proponents of Block 77 were convinced the Municipal Building block would act as a magnet for development. It was purposely situated in an area as yet underdeveloped commercially. The reason was not cost alone, though that certainly was a factor. This area, it was said again and again, would inevitably fill with large business blocks—first to office the lawyers, accountants, and others associated with the business of the city and county, then to serve the ancillary needs of those employed in the Municipal Building. The result would be concentric rings of development ultimately connecting to the Nicollet Avenue axis of downtown business.

Such a development never occurred. But the vision of a secondary hub of Minneapolis commerce helped the project survive the unanticipated economic hardships of the 1890s. The cost of so great a municipal structure became an increasingly heavy burden for city and county taxpayers as the area plunged in 1893 from building boom to far-reaching depression. Yet new bond issues were required as the costs leapt beyond the initial appropriation. What the Municipal Building would do for Minneapolis development was the carrot dangled before the business community, the great equalizer that would turn the extravagant civic monument into an instrument of economic well-being.

The list of modern megablocks following the same carrot is endless. The Nicollet Hotel of 1924 and the Metrodome of 1982 are only the most conspicuous examples. But as the past hundred years have shown, carrots made of granite are seldom in danger of being eaten. No project has succeeded in creating an expanding hub of development off the Nicollet-Marquette trunk. The boosters of the municipal block invented a model for downtown development that has lived to a ripe old age quite independent of reality.

The great visions that made the Municipal Building possible were one with the myths common to the burgeoning metropolises of the upper plains in the latter part of the nineteenth century. Cities such as Minneapolis, which had no significant past, easily absorbed the historical associations their monuments brought with them. No one could tell what Minneapolis or Des Moines or Omaha or Kansas City might become, so each city thought of itself as a new Chicago. The Minneapolis building boom was for several years the most intense in the country, so it seemed natural that all the new pockets of development within a mile of either bank of the Mississippi River would meld into one great business center.

Associating the popular will and the rule of law with castles and cathedrals of another time, conjuring Minneapolis alongside New York and Chicago, and seeing the downtown spill out over the plains were all myths about the past and future. Subsequent history has given them short shrift. Yet without their primary force, many of the courageous decisions that moved the city forward might never have been made—among them the decision to build the Municipal Building as it is today.

The Minneapolis Brewing Company was one of several in the Twin Cities to build megablock developments.

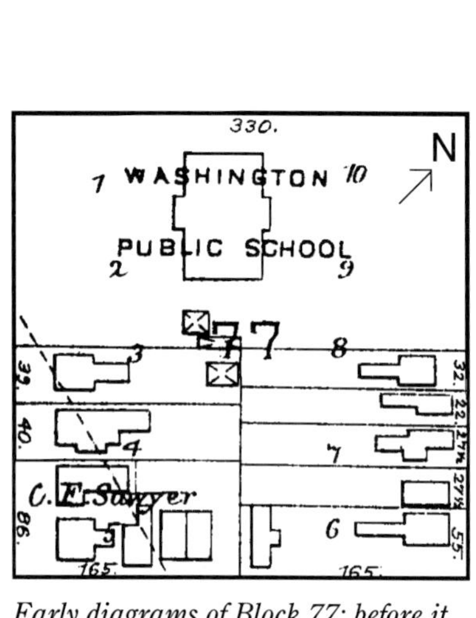

Early diagrams of Block 77: before it was purchased for the site of the new Municipal Building (above) and in its larger setting in 1892 (right).

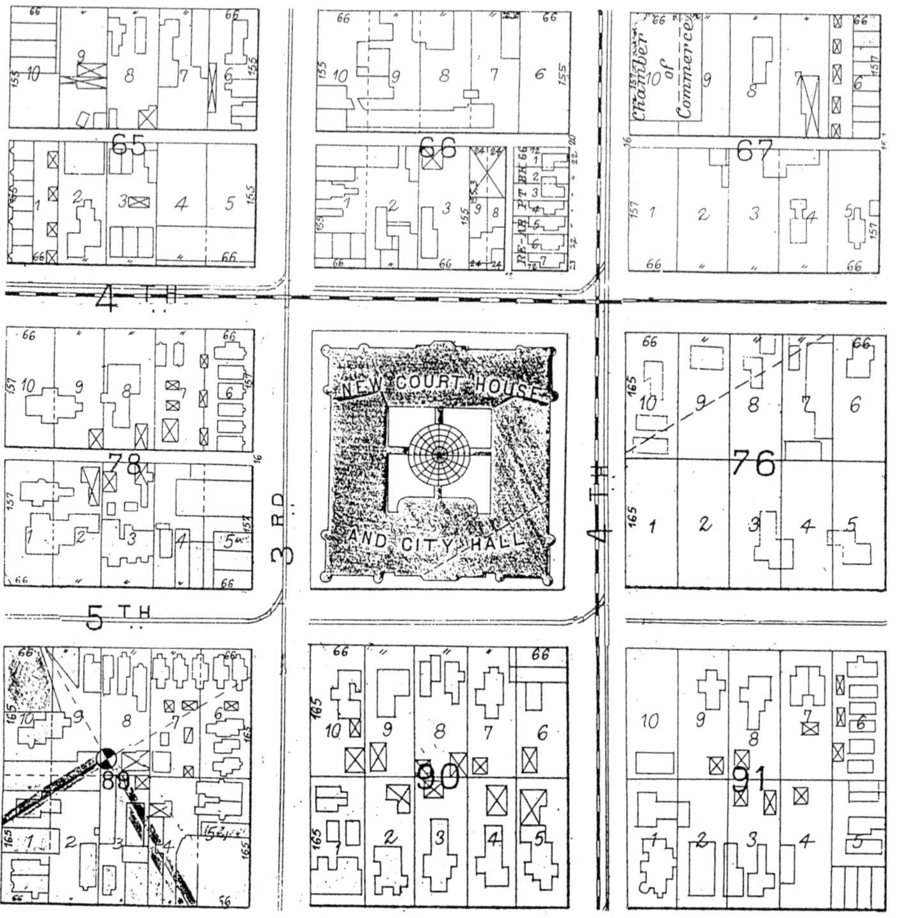

The Social and Economic Climate

Minneapolis and Hennepin County formally decided to erect a new courthouse and city hall in 1887, a year without spectacular events locally or worldwide. Lacking any single device to inflame the public imagination, the newspapers served up a concoction of intoxicating anticipations and dreadful rumors. On the international front, Queen Victoria's reign had reached a fifty-year milestone, and anticipation of the Jubilee celebration—scheduled for June 22—spread through the part of the world that felt the hand of the British Empire. Glaring at the party plans were headlines pronouncing the inevitability of war in continental Europe, involving Russia, Austria, France, and the countries between. Peace broke out instead; the rumor mill had to look elsewhere for grist.

American news swung on the same pendulum, with gaiety and gloom more clearly divided along social and economic lines. Life at the top was perfectly captured in a widely reported February White House reception, at which two women of renowned wealth, Mrs. Leland Stanford and Mrs. Frank Leslie, engaged in a duel of diamonds, battling for the choicest spot under the chandeliers. The *Boston Record* claimed that a million dollars hung on the ears and necks of the two women, while the *Baltimore American* decried the display of "necks, arms, and busts" in general.

There was the underside of society as well. Laboring people smarted under wages that failed to keep pace with the tremendous growth in national wealth of the mid-1880s. In 1886, the Haymarket Riot in Chicago had led to the bombing death of seven policemen during a confrontation with anarchists. A stigma of violence and subversion attached to the labor movement in general. The Chicago riot was a front-page fixture for much of 1887, and the question of the fate of the anarchists fueled hot dispute until the leaders were executed at the end of the year.

Both these themes, of wealth on display and labor under protest, were exploited by the news-hungry Minneapolis papers, but in a spirit a bit brighter and less dividing. Minneapolis was enjoying one of the greatest building booms in the country, and the city was buoyed by a spirit of boosterism and civic pride largely canceling the worst effects of the widening gulf between rich and poor. The titans of the city—the flour-milling Pillsburys and Washburns and speculator Louis Menage, for instance—carried out their enterprises with considerably less self-display than their eastern counterparts, devoting public energies to projects of genuine benefit to the city. Without the enthusiastic support and volunteer efforts of the Minneapolis upper crust, so ambitious a scheme as the Municipal Building would scarcely have been considered.

Even more important, the economic prospects of laborers and mechanics were supported at nearly every turn (there were some setbacks) by a generosity born of the pervading spirit of optimism regarding the city's immediate future. In April 1887, the city council approved with little debate a request from the stonemasons' union that only union masons be hired for city projects. Later that month, a motion for an eight-hour day for all laborers employed in public works was soundly defeated, sent to special committee, returned to full council, and passed. Though it was not put into effect as stipulated, that an eight-hour bill got so far in city government put Minneapolis into the vanguard of progressive labor.

Even the Haymarket Riot in Chicago, which the Minneapolis press milked for all its worth, was treated as somebody else's news. In October, the national meetings of the Knights of Labor convened in Minneapolis, and a resolution condemning the death sentence of the Chicago anarchists—a moderate resolution, considering the hysteria surrounding their trial—was hotly debated and defeated. A *Minneapolis Tribune* editorial on November 12 assured readers that though several hundred avowed anarchists might be in the city, "they are not, presumably, intending any mischief, and they will feel the wholesome influence of the Chicago executions."

Automated mass transit promised a means of providing cheap and ready means for workers to get to their jobs. The electric trolley had just been invented in Atlanta and would soon make its debut in Minneapolis. A group of local entrepreneurs was also trying to whip up public interest in a subway system. By December, they had gotten far enough to incorporate as the "Minneapolis Subway Company" with a projected capital stock of $500,000.

Finally, among government leaders a strong current of populism linked the interests of all sectors of the population. In a move that was perhaps more symbolic than realistic, incoming Mayor Albert A. Ames recommended to the city council in 1887 that "all the ordinances except those containing vested rights be repealed, and that new ones containing plain English and divested of legal verbiage be enacted in their stead . . . All laws should be so framed and worded that the humblest citizen might be able to read and understand them."

Fifth Street has seen a procession of "skyscrapers"—(proceeding from the foreground) the Municipal Building (1889-1906), the Telephone Building (1931), and Opus Corporation (1985 and 1989)—but it has not become the hub of downtown Minneapolis.

The local newspapers reported a number of social and environmental ills. Cigarette-making was decried as a national waste, with twice the money expended on schools going up in recreational smoke. Pornography was barely existent as a commercial enterprise, but fortune-telling and astrology raised some of the same issues, particularly in their effect on the local business climate. Minneapolis dealt with the problem in modern fashion, by passing a licensing ordinance with a fee so steep as to force fortune-tellers and astrologers out of business. They were required to pay $1,000 annually, ten times that required of peddlers and forty times the fee to operate a lane of bowling.

Industrial pollution was a growing concern, with passage of an ordinance declaring the "emission of dense smoke from our smoke stacks and chimneys a nuisance" and laying stiff fines on those who failed to comply. The ordinance was short-lived. It was repealed on grounds anticipating dozens of court cases in the 1960s and 1970s: "There are yet no appliances known and in use that can be relied upon to consume or prevent the emission of dense smoke at certain times without a large increase in the expense of fuel or loss of power and injury to boilers."

The Need for a New Municipal Building

In 1887, the city's most important civic buildings presented a sorry contrast to the clusters of solid business blocks filling its downtown grid. The old courthouse, an 1857 structure on Eighth Avenue (now Chicago) and Fourth Street, had been built in a primitive version of the Greek Revival mode. At the time of construction it was far and away the most lavishly designed and built structure in the county. In fact, its $40,000 price tag had created a public storm and inspired endless repetitions of the claim that the county would not need so large a building for half a decade. But by the 1870s, its size and inefficient plan had already begun to stunt county legal and judicial processes. Judges, county officers, and employees were severely crowded. Lawyers and businessmen complained of its distance from the downtown core. The jail and sheriff's residence

The county courthouse built in 1857 could barely be seen for the trees by 1875. The jail and sheriff's residence are at right.

built ten years later immediately south of the old courthouse, was even more vulnerable to criticism. One local wag said its "architecture does not resemble anything on earth, or the waters under the earth or the heavens above."

The old city hall on Bridge Square (where Hennepin Avenue joined Nicollet) scored higher on both aesthetic and utilitarian grounds, but its day was approaching. Its once-convenient location halfway between old St. Anthony across the river and the new Minneapolis downtown had become a bottleneck several blocks removed from the center of current downtown development. Furthermore, its top-heavy 1873 Second Empire styling, crudely rendered in local limestone, smacked more of a prairie town overreaching itself than of a city boasting solid accomplishment. Ventilation was so poor that postal clerks on the ground floor swooned from sewage fumes; nothing within the stone walls could prevent a firestorm.

City Hall, built in 1873 and shown here about 1875, was unsafe for employees by the mid-1880s.

For all the inadequacies of the old structures, local officials at both city and county levels were loath to be involved in a building project that would apply so immediate and large a tax burden as construction on a new site. But by the middle of 1886, even the taxpayers were beginning to grumble openly about the shabby state of county offices and services.

The first effect of the growing public interest in a new courthouse was to bring back the fight of 1856 about where the building should be. The laboring classes favored rebuilding on the old site because of the increased expense of acquiring and clearing a new one. They were joined by many of the southsiders, who wanted to keep the building close to the residential center of the city; some of these were willing to settle for a move closer to downtown, but not beyond Third Avenue South. Finally, the uptowners and businessmen were keen on a location somewhere on Nicollet or Hennepin.

Among the city's commercial interests, only one body came out against any new building whatever, and that was the Board of Trade. Board members Judge Isaac Atwater (soon to write a copious history of Hennepin County) and lumberman J. B. Bassett both looked askance at any new building scheme. They were skeptical of the economic boom and unwilling to tie municipal expenses to an assumption it would continue.

In the meantime, the Hennepin County Bar Association was rapidly establishing itself as the leader in the agitation for a new courthouse. Under the leadership of P. M. Babcock, the association drew up a draft of a bill intended for the 1887 session of the state legislature. Presented to the county board for approval on January 10, 1887, the bill's most important provisions were the raising of a bond for $1,500,000 to build a county courthouse and the establishment of a five-man building commission independent of the county board. Commission members were to be George Pillsbury, O. E. Merriman, John Crosby, E. M. Wilson, and Thomas Lowry.

The bar association proposal delicately sidestepped the location debate by assigning site selection, condemnation, and appraisal to the building commission. At first, this move simply exchanged one furor for another, especially among those who felt their base of power threatened. The county commissioners were incensed at having a job passed to someone else the instant it was created. The city council, which so far was not even involved in the matter, decided on principle to side with the county commissioners. Political bosses

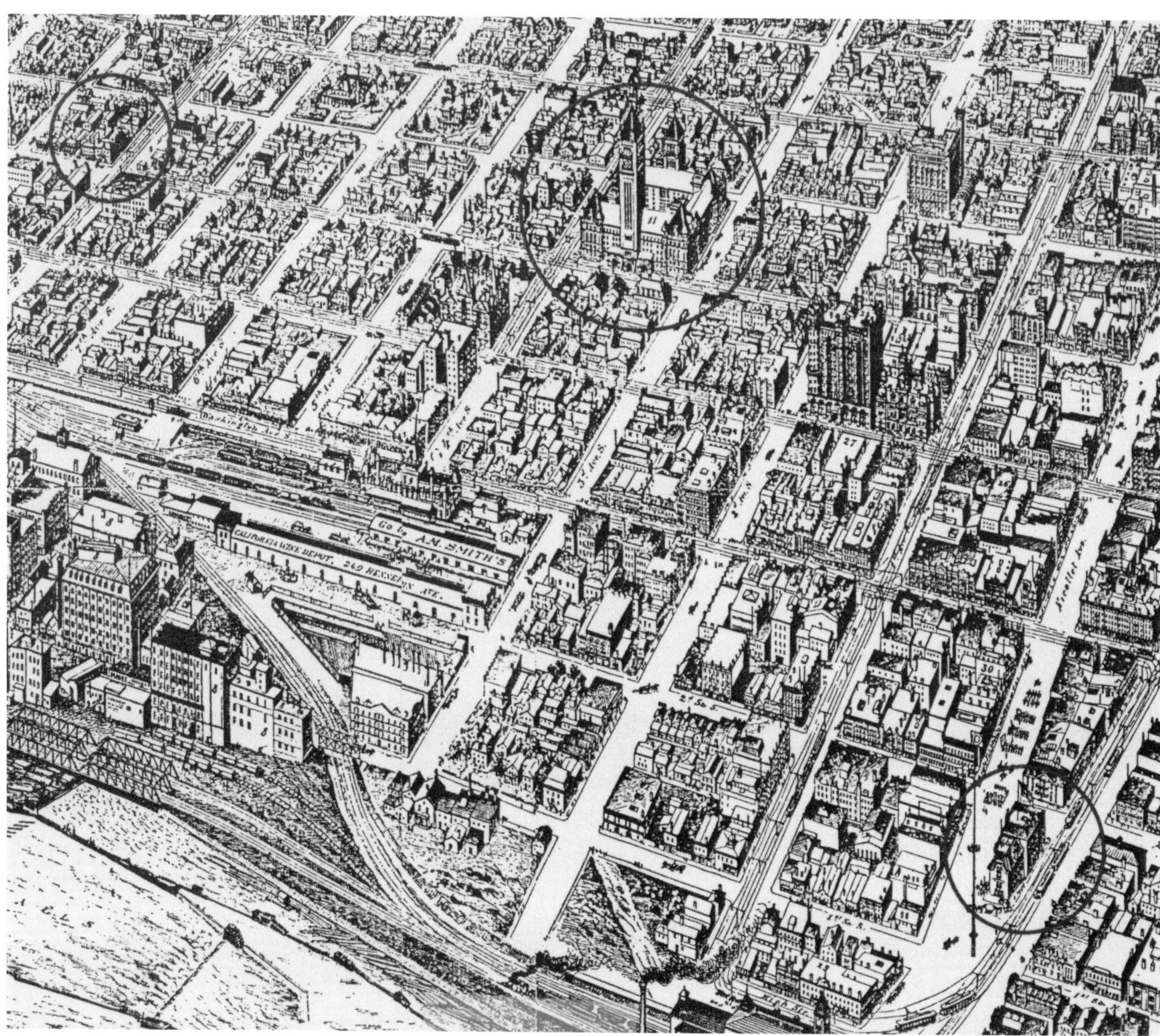

This 1891 bird's-eye view of the city of Minneapolis shows the old county courthouse (left circle) and city hall (lower right circle) as well as the new Municipal Building (center) bringing the two governments under one roof.

of all persuasions feared the new commission because its nonpartisan composition would make it hard to manipulate. Even labor organizers took issue with the building commission proposal, for quite a different reason: they saw it as one more instance of the city's interests being represented and controlled by appointment from the top, this time by the state legislature and its appointees.

Most of these objections, however, came from the officials of local government, politics, and labor. The media and the business community were outspoken in their support of a building commission and seemed to have the majority of the citizenry behind them. At issue was not only the independence of the commission from political manipulation but also its stability through a decade or more of local elections.

On the issue of joining a city hall to the county building, the bar association was at first noncommittal. The idea of erecting a combination structure was still a novelty in many communities, and Minneapolis had the added obstacle of already having reached its 5-percent limit of bond indebtedness. The bar association simply recommended that the city council appoint a committee to confer with the county commissioners about housing the two governments under one roof. After the proposal had aired for a few weeks, the association convened on January 24 and 25 in a pair of exhaustive debates regarding all the publicly contested points. The meetings ended in consensus on all the points of the initial presentation plus one. That the new courthouse be combined with a city hall apparently had reached broad acceptance among local government officials.

Prominent Minneapolis miller and financier Curtis H. Pettit is generally credited with making the conjunction of city and county offices into a workable scheme. After his election to the Minnesota legislature, he enlisted the help of city attorney Judson N. Cross to draft a bill melding the concerns of city councilmen and county commissioners—mostly to do with financing and the structuring of the city-county relationship—with the proposals of the bar association. This draft was identical to that ultimately enacted by the legislature on all but one point: the number of commissioners swelled from five to nine.

Curtis H. Pettit

The Court House and City Hall Act of March 2, 1887

In the meantime, the Minnesota legislature had convened, and the "Hennepin County Legislative Delegation" already had its hands full: Franklin Avenue and Twentieth Avenue North needed bridges, the city needed a board of public works and a police commission, and it needed redistricting and extended city limits. And the county commissioners and county attorney needed relief from their inadequate incomes.

To make matters worse, the Municipal Building bill was referred to the Hennepin delegation just as the question of moving the capital from St. Paul to Minneapolis put in its annual appearance. The enthusiasm of the Minneapolis representatives about that possibility was as predictable as it was blinding to other concerns.

Still the miracle occurred. Between February 5, when the city hall and courthouse bill was introduced, and February 25, the Hennepin delegation waded through all its political agenda, the house killed the capital proposition, and under Pettit's insistent leadership the bill was reported back to the full house, where it immediately passed. Three days later, it passed the senate, and on March 2, 1887, the last day of the session, it received the signature of Governor Andrew R. McGill. So began the political process that was to culminate in a public monument more costly and permanent than even the most enthusiastic of its early champions envisioned.

H. H. Richardson's architecture, particularly his Allegheny County Buildings in Pittsburgh, served as a source of inspiration for many architects submitting entries in competition for the design of the Minneapolis Municipal Building. Richardson was the first American to devise an architectural style. His adaptation of French Romanesque architecture to modern tastes and requirements was a powerful expression of the robust spirit of late-nineteenth-century America. Many of his buildings were widely imitated, and the Richardsonian Romanesque style enjoyed a decade of enormous popularity from 1885 to 1895.

Planning the Monument

Enabling legislation for the new Municipal Building was officially known as "Chapter 395, Special Laws of 1887." Though drawn up in haste and pushed through with a minimum of deliberation, it proved a wonderfully workable document, the backbone for all work on the Municipal Building for twenty years. The key provisions of the 1887 act were:

- designation of the whole of Block 77 as the site
- appointment of a Board of Court House and City Hall Commissioners with three county commissioners, three city councilmen, and three prominent citizens outside municipal government
- authorization of the board to purchase and condemn properties as required and the transfer of the west half of the block from the Minneapolis Board of Education to the Board of Commissioners
- erection of a new building with "architectural symmetry" and divided into a city and a county component
- authorization of a bond issue for $1,500,000.

The act also introduced a convenient abbreviation of "The Hennepin County Court House and Minneapolis City Hall" into "The Municipal Building."

The bland, legal language of these provisions gave little hint of the painstaking deliberations that had created them. The most important concerned the creation of the Board of Commissioners. At first slated to include five members, the board was almost doubled, to draw into the process partisans with power enough to stall the project if left outside.

The choice of the county commissioners to serve on the board brought organized labor directly into the fold. John Swift was an officer of the Knights of Labor, and Oliver T. Erickson was a carpenter and exponent of the eight-hour day. Erickson's knowledge of building practices soon led to a long stint as "clerk of the works," with the responsibility of overseeing construction on the new building. The third county commissioner chosen, William S. Chowen, was the token and obligatory rural representative.

The Board of Commissioners (above), reported the Minneapolis Tribune in 1895, "was as representative a body of all the prominent political interests in Minneapolis at that time as could have been selected." Washburn was its first president.

The city council representatives showed a different kind of mix. David M. Clough and Lars Swenson were both state senators as well as councilmen. Though C. H. Pettit and the others who had selected the commissioners had probably not anticipated it, these two would prove ready allies of Erickson and Swift, creating a backbone of labor support that would give the fiscal conservatives sleepless nights. Clough was a particularly astute choice because of his membership on the state's Republican Central Committee; he had recently served as president of the city council and was well known as one of the city's leading lumberman. He would become president of the board for a brief period before being elected attorney general and rising to the governorship in 1895. Swenson was a Swedish immigrant currently serving as treasurer of Augsburg College. He had a reputation for reliability and a way of keeping things brief and to the point; he served as treasurer of the board until his death in 1904. The final city council representative was its standing president, Titus Marek. He was a Democrat, a rare species in the current city government.

Finally, the three members-at-large each had important constituencies and an active voice in public affairs: Charles M. Loring was president of the Minneapolis Park Board, Swiss-born John C. Oswald was a state senator and the other token Democrat, and William D. Washburn had recently been elected to the U.S. Senate. Washburn's government service and other responsibilities, including directorship of Pillsbury-Washburn Flour Mills, kept him from attending to much of the detail of the new board's work; but as a man renowned for skillful and pragmatic handling of complex and controversial issues, his election as first president of the Board of Commissioners was assured.

The choice of Block 77 represented a compromise between the "uptowners," the "downtowners," and the southsiders. Bounded on the northeast and southwest by Fourth and Fifth streets respectively, the block was equidistant from the old settlement near the river and the rapidly developing Hennepin-Nicollet axis. Its detachment by several blocks from either one of these commercial development areas caused some grumbling among businesspeople, but everyone seemed convinced the city would expand to the east in the near future. That half the block was already owned by the city was an added attraction; although the Board of Education had to be compensated, its cooperation was assured, and avoiding legal battles was at least as important as keeping purchase costs to a minimum.

Even the supposed price tag of the building project was fraught with political implications. The $1,500,000 figure (including lot and building) had never been exposed to public scrutiny nor debated among the various interests in the project. How the author of the figure, the Hennepin County Bar Association, arrived at that amount is uncertain. Yet there it was, presented without argument in January, voted into the enabling legislation without debate in February, and signed into law in March. Later developments made it clear the price tag was little more than a guess, allowed to float along lest any barrier to the pell-mell course of the bill allow labor agitators, the recalcitrant Board of Trade, or any other citizens' group to stall the act.

Washington School, shown in about 1880, occupied part of the Municipal Building site when it was purchased in 1887.

Purchasing the Site

The first charge of the Board of Commissioners was to purchase all of the properties on Block 77. The west half, owned by the Board of Education from the earliest days of the city, had in 1856 become the site of Union School, the first public schoolhouse in Minneapolis west of the Mississippi River. When Union School burned in 1865, it was immediately replaced by Washington School, an imposing three-story structure of local limestone built in much the same Frontier French style as the old city hall.

From a political standpoint, this was the easiest part of the Municipal Building site to clear, as it was owned by a city agency and its only improvements (the school itself and a quaint wooden bell tower dating to Union School days) were already perceived as outmoded. In June 1887, the Board of Commissioners purchased the site for $165,000.

The remainder of the block was occupied by twelve frame houses owned by seven separate parties, few of whom lived on the premises. Immediately after reaching agreement on the school property purchase, the Board of Commissioners offered to buy the privately held properties at $400 per front foot, $100 a foot less than the Board of Education had received for its parcel. When the owners balked, the Board of Commissioners ordered condemnation proceedings. Prices were eventually set by three board-appointed appraisers acting on the testimony of four expert witnesses. By late September the Board of Commissioners had all the private properties in hand. The $400 figure stood as the norm, with some adjustment for the density of development on the block. After dickering with three of the owners, the board negotiated a final price for all of the southeast half of Block 77 of $161,659, just a few thousand dollars less than the school half of the block.

Only when the site purchases were complete did the Board of Commissioners turn to the matter of design. This was typical of how the board handled all business concerning the project: methodically, one step at a time, leaving no stone unturned that might provoke legal battles or escalate costs. William Washburn, the board's first president, was the chief instigator of this policy. "We have to spend a large amount of money," he said, "and it is best for us to go slow and sure. We want to be sure that each step taken is the right one."

Opening the Competition

In November 1887, John De Laittre announced to the Board of Commissioners: "If I had a building to put up I would tell Fred Kees about what I wanted and ask him to make sketch plans until he suited me, and then when I was suited I would tell him to go ahead and superintend the building at the usual percentage to architects." Eighteen meetings, six months, and pages of bad press later, his fellow commissioners may have wished they had gone that route.

De Laittre had just been appointed chairman of the construction committee in the wake of Charles Loring's resignation. His career mirrored that of C. H. Pettit, who had introduced the authorizing legislation for the Municipal Building. Like Pettit, he had established himself in manufacturing and lumbering as well as finance and banking, had turned to politics in midlife, and had developed an active interest in penal institutions.

De Laittre was an astute enough politician to know that what he could or would do as a businessman would not wash in the planning of the Municipal Building. He quickly acknowledged that the Municipal Building was "a public affair," and that simply appointing an architect was not the "regular way."

The regular way was open competition, in which any architect could submit plans, a few would be awarded prizes, and all but one would go away kicking himself for devoting so much money and office time to an enterprise offering so slight a chance of return. On November 7, the construction committee presented its first draft of an "advertisement for architects." Though it was soon supplanted by a more detailed version, it perfectly captured the commissioners' early vision of the Municipal Building.

To Minneapolis Architects

The sum appropriated for said building will be $1,200,000. The main front will be on Fourth Street, but entrances are desired on all four sides. The exterior will show as one building, construction to be of some economical but durable stone, and entirely fireproof; no wood used in construction except room floors, door and window frames and finish; the interior lighted from an open court, so the interior rooms will be light; one-half to be used as a courthouse, ample for all purposes for the next 50 years; the other part to be for a city hall, with room for the different boards and all departments of city government, suitable in size and convenience for a city of from 500,000 to 750,000 inhabitants. Particular attention is called to ventilation, sewage, heating, and light; both parts to be heated, and power for elevator service to be obtained from one central plant located in basement; access to basement to be by some underground roadway for wagons, so as not to disfigure the grounds surrounding.

The first draft was directed to Minneapolis architects in a pointed effort by De Laittre's committee to contain the selection process. But the chairman refused to go along. For all his misgivings about competitive process, De Laittre believed the competition should be opened to all. So he refused to sign the first draft of the call for plans. The commission voted to adopt it over his objections, with his the only dissenting vote.

That was not the end of the matter. After some jawboning by De Laittre, a greatly expanded version of the advertisement was considered on November

16. This general "Notice to Architects" read without reference to the location of their offices. It was quickly approved, immediately published in a brochure, and circulated to the architectural press.

The published advertisement added considerable detail to the earlier draft. It identified the Fourth Street entrance, for example, as the principal one on account of its "easterly front" (though it was really northeasterly and more north than east)and specified that if the entrances were treated unequally, that entry must be most highly ornamented. A second change made quality and durability, rather than economy, the first priority in choice of stone. Both these changes figured prominently in the design and construction of the building.

The change with the greatest immediate effect was the advertisement's elaboration of the specifications and award system for entries. All submissions were to consist of four scaled elevations or two elevations and one perspective, a sectional view of the building, and floor plans for each story and basement. Each was to be accompanied by an estimate of construction costs. Five prizes ranging from $1,500 to $400 were to be awarded , with the Board of Commissioners retaining the right to award the prizes and reject all the plans.

Response from the regional architectural community was immediate and hostile. For several years, the American Institute of Architects and its offshoot, the Western Association of Architects, had fought against such competitions as an insult to the profession. "The gentlemen who have issued this fine brochure upon architectural practice" drew a particularly sarcastic assessment from the editor of the Chicago-based *Inland Architect and News Record:* "They are, presumably, business men, and it is fair to suppose they do not believe that architects are different from the rest of mankind, and work for love, live on air and never pay their help."

Officially sanctioned animosity toward the competition kept all of the larger eastern firms and all but four of the Chicago firms from entering. Architects willing to take a long shot at the competition were hamstrung by the two-month deadline, requiring all plans to be in by January 16, 1888. Even local architects, who everybody believed would receive preferential treatment, balked. L. S. Buffington, the city's first architect to rise to eminence, was conspicuously silent, though at least one preliminary sketch for the project survives among his papers. The only apparently negotiable item was the deadline. On this point, the Board of Commissioners was soon forced to budge by several letters of protest from prominent architects. The upshot was an extension to February 15 of that year.

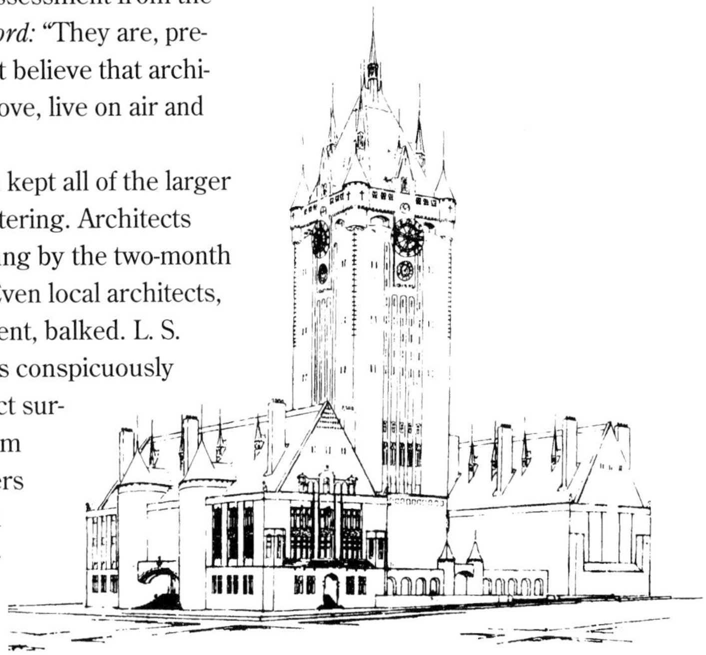

L. S. Buffington did a preliminary sketch but declined to enter the competition for design of the Municipal Building.

Despite hardship imposed by the conditions of the competition, many architects responded: 250 wrote for further specifications, and twenty-seven sent in complete designs, with two submitting a pair. Twenty-six of the twenty-nine were ruled complete; of these, ten were from Minneapolis, four from St. Paul, and four from Chicago.

The newly formed Minneapolis partnership of Appleyard and Dorr was the first entrant. Most of the other Minneapolis participants were young but established firms: the prolific J. and A. Haley, Maine natives G. W. and F. D. Orff, French-trained W. H. Dennis and Company, W. D. Kimball and Company, F. E. Hoover, Scottish stonemason-turned-architect Alexander Murrie, and the meteor among local firms, Long and Kees. All of these had fielded major commercial commissions in the building boom of 1883 to 1886. Yost Brothers, a new partnership spanning Minneapolis and Columbus, Ohio, also responded. The final Minneapolis entrant was Isaac Hodgson and Son, an Indianapolis transplant boasting the only extensive civic building experience. The elder Hodgson had designed several county courthouses in Indiana before arriving in Minnesota. Two of these buildings remain among the premier architectural monuments of that state.

St. Paul's entrants were, by contrast, nearly all novices, with little capacity to supervise or even produce full working drawings. Omeyer and Thori were gifted draftsmen at the dawn of an illustrious partnership; they had a tiny office and were barely embarked on their first important commissions. C. B. Seaton had recently launched what would be an exceptionally obscure career, and Lyman Farwell and Henry Maltby were still only apprentices. The soon-to-be illustrious Cass Gilbert was conspicuously silent, as were his prolific colleague and friend Clarence Johnston and St. Paul's other young leading architect, Allen H. Stem.

John De Laittre was chairman of the construction committee during the design competition.

Architects responding from Chicago fell into no clear pattern. Mifflin E. Bell had recently set up an independent practice after an erratic and controversial tenure in the Office of the Supervising Architect of the United States Treasury, where he had responsibility for all the nation's federal buildings. Edbrooke and Burnham was a well-established firm with a sound regional reputation; Handy and Cady, though less prominent, belonged in the same category, while the firm of Cole and Dahlgren was practically unknown, even in Chicago. The *Minneapolis Tribune* reported a fifth Chicago entry, Burnham and Root, probably the most esteemed midwestern firm of the time, but its entry is not corroborated by any other sources. This company had recently won the competition (done under American Institute of Architects guidelines) for the Board of Trade of Kansas City.

New York, Boston, Philadelphia, and Washington, D.C., the country's eastern hubs of architectural practice, sent two entries among them, an appropriately named W. L. Minor of Boston, and trainee Charles F. Collum of Philadelphia. Two remaining entries came from Detroit, and one each from Pittsburgh, Louisville, San Francisco, Birmingham, and North Swenson, Maine.

The pattern that emerged from all of this was quite clear. In Minneapolis, most of the architectural firms with a shot at the prize entered the competition. Otherwise, the entrants fell into two classes, at the extreme ends of qualification and experience. Half of the architects were novices with little to lose; the other half had established repertoires in public building design and were able to submit variations of already executed work. Apart from the Chicago firms that have already been mentioned, the McDonald Brothers of Louisville, Kentucky, clearly fell into the latter category, making similar ventures into Kansas, Iowa, and Nebraska, several of which met with success. Even more successful was the firm of Colonel E. E. Myers and Sons, originally of Detroit, which must have set a standard for mobility in the 1880s. Brief sojourns in Dallas, Des Moines, Omaha, and Detroit, had equipped the colonel with "thirty-five years experience, and those, gentlemen, spent entirely upon the execution of just such important work."

Selecting the Architect

In mid-February, two rooms were rented in the lavishly remodeled Boston Block for display of the "show-drawings" of twenty-three of the submitted designs. The exhibit received little local press, though from an artistic standpoint it was a sensational showing of architectural draftsmanship.

Several competitors totally ignored a competition guideline discouraging color renderings. Handy and Cady hired Paul Lautrup, the preeminent free-

Though the competition drawings immediately became the property of the Board of Commissioners, all were discarded but the elevation, plan, and section drawings of the winning entry, which eventually passed to the Hennepin County Historical Society. Other entries exist only in the black-and-white publication of a handful of the perspective drawings in architectural periodicals and the local Real Estate Review. Handy and Cady submitted the two designs at left: one English Jacobean (top), the other Florentine Renaissance (bottom).

W. H. Dennis and Company's second-place rendering (right) was almost a copy of H. H. Richardson's Allegheny Courthouse (see page 14). McDonald Brothers also submitted a Richardsonian Romanesque design (below).

lance architectural renderer of Chicago, and he gave them sun-drenched watercolors worthy of the firm's two designs, one Florentine Renaissance with a Venetian tower and the other English Jacobean. Not to be outdone, Long and Kees retained the services of the chief draftsman for the *American Architect,* David A. Gregg, for a clean pen-and-ink rendering of a Romanesque design, then coupled this entry with a watercolor sketch by Chicago artist J. K. Wilson of a neoclassical H-plan.

Minneapolis artists also got a chance to show what they could do. John Anderson ("the divine Anderson" according to *Northwestern Architect*, the leading architectural periodical of the region) was the most renowned talent in the city before Buffington pulled in the brilliant Harvey Ellis. W. H. Dennis enlisted Anderson for a sepia pen-and-ink drawing and two watercolor perspectives, splashing flowers as well as sunlight around its Romanesque design. Finally, Orff Brothers had just added the *Northwestern Architect*'s chief renderer, Francis W. Fitzpatrick, to its staff, and he made a suitably murky watercolor rendering of the firm's French Renaissance design in a winter setting. One architectural reporter thought this the outstanding design and rendering in the competition.

Of the twenty-six complete plans submitted, fully two-thirds were in the monumental Romanesque style of H. H. Richardson, and at least two of these—one by Long and Kees and one by W. H. Dennis—were unabashed adaptations of Richardson's Allegheny County Courthouse in Pittsburgh. Alexander Murrie's design was a faithful adaptation of the Renaissance Revival Glasgow City Hall, which the architect had worked on while still a master stonemason in Scotland. The others ranged the spectrum of styles. E. E. Myers' entry, the most praised and most vilified of all the series, was facetiously described as in the "bamboo fishing rod style" because of numerous turrets and piers with periodic bulges.

However open to satire some of the entries were, the Board of Commissioners had several strong designs to draw from. During the last two weeks of February, competition was narrowed to eleven entries, six from Minneapolis architects. Then the commissioners got stuck. Whether they were unable to reach a consensus or were becoming aware of the minefield through which they walked, they decided not to go it alone. After their frantic call to Chicago, architect W. W. Boyington agreed to select the winning designs from among the eleven finalists.

On March 1, Boyington stepped off the train and into a nightmare. His task was to review the eleven final designs for floor space, room arrangement, light, mechanical systems, cost effectiveness, and artistic quality. Then he was to rank the top five. For this task he was given four days. As might be expected, the slate that Boyington came up with pleased nobody. His first two choices were out-of-towners, and each of these had designed buildings well beyond the stipulated budget.

M. E. Bell was given first position, and his design was projected to cost at least $2,000,000. The second-place design, by E. E. Myers and Sons, carried a price tag of $3,224,500. Third place went to Long and Kees, the only firm among the final eleven that had taken the specifications into consideration. Fourth went to Murrie and fifth to Dennis, their designs also projected in excess of $1,200,000.

At a subsequent meeting, Boyington switched the third and fifth places without providing an explanation, moving Dennis on up the ladder and Long and Kees down. At this point, the newspapers and architectural press added to the confusion by reporting that Boyington had recommended W. H. Dennis and Company for the first prize, which, given board pressures, may actually have been the truth.

Alexander Murrie's English Renaissance design (left) took the fourth-place prize. Yost Brothers submitted a Richardsonian design (above), which the Inland Architect reported to be "colossal in all its details," but it did not place in the competition.

By the time the Board of Commissioners had released Boyington from his misery, the midwestern architectural world was in an uproar. Boyington was trounced by his colleagues as an accomplice in an unholy ritual. Critics had a hard time deciding which to kick the hardest: the Board of Commissioners bringing in a last-minute expert and playing politics with his selections or an architect agreeing to play instant expert and proceeding to recommend two atrociously overblown designs.

The reputation of the Board of Commissioners was not aided by its failure to have met as an entire body since late January. Two missing commissioners finally returned to town in early April, and the board called a special meeting on April 13 to gauge where everyone stood. Even then, the commissioners decided to put off the decision for another month, allowing time for two more outside experts to provide cost estimates of the five best plans.

At the regular May meeting, the estimates were read, and the board commenced balloting. Boyington's five favorites were still the finalists, but the Long and Kees Romanesque plan had been exchanged for the firm's less-expensive neoclassical H-plan. Apparently, Long and Kees' friends on the board thought the substitution would improve the architects' chance for the prize. But when balloting commenced, Long and Kees appeared to be out of the picture. Thirty-two formal ballots were taken at the May meeting, with the first and last an identical deadlock between W. H. Dennis and E. E. Myers and Son. Once more the decision was deferred.

Long and Kees submitted two designs. The H-plan Italian Renaissance palazzo (right) took first place in the competition.

By June 5, when the board finally made its decision, the question had broken decisively in favor of Long and Kees. There can be little doubt about what happened. The architects apparently, on invitation or through impatience, had begun to do a bit of arm-twisting. Fred Kees had a stalwart champion in the person of De Laittre, and both Long and Kees were masters at political suasion. Kees had earlier parlayed his membership at First Baptist Church into one of the grandest commissions in the city, and Long had donated a large sum to the Library Board en route to winning the competition for design of the Minneapolis Public Library for the partnership. The editor of the *Inland Architect* assured his readers that only "a Napoleon of architectural business tactics" could win such a competition, and the *Northwestern Architect,* which would soon welcome Kees to its staff, asserted that the final decision "was merely a matter of wire-pulling, and the most astute wire pullers won."

Long and Kees had also won points with some commissioners because of their solo effort to adapt their plans—both of them—to the specifications of the circular. This enhanced their already favorable local reputation as good businessmen who would see their plans through. The upshot was a first ballot that gave Long and Kees four votes, one short of the majority needed; the remaining votes were scattered. On the third ballot, a fifth member came aboard, and the Long and Kees firm was in. Only the president of the Board of Commissioners, William Washburn, was publicly displeased with the result. He continued to cast his vote for Mifflin Bell as an expression of protest that the Long and Kees H-plan "had been ignored by the expert employed by the commission."

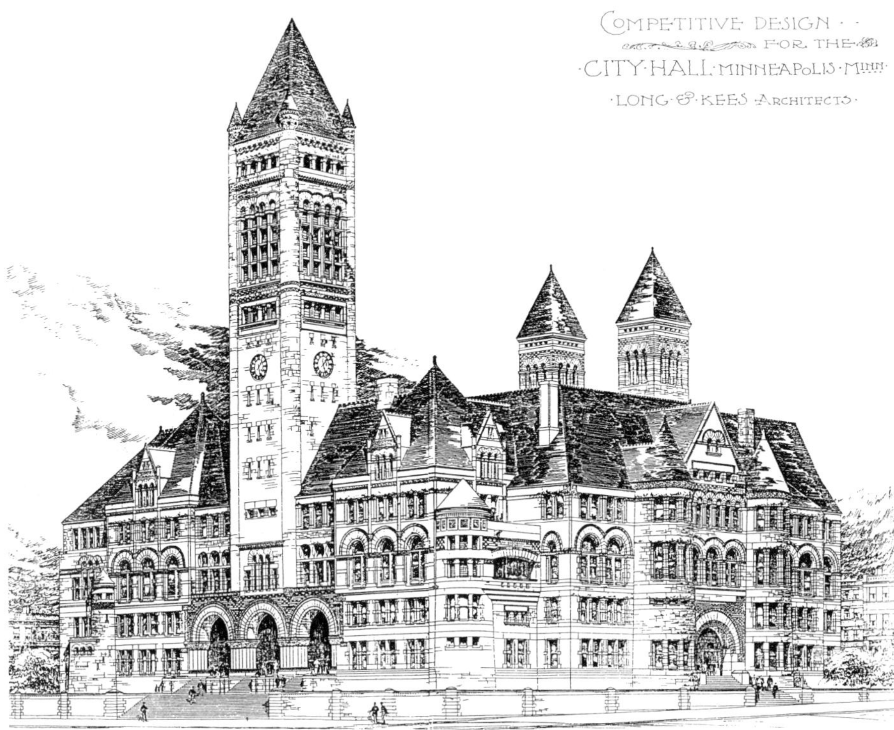

A second Long and Kees submission (left), an adaptation of Richardson's Allegheny Courthouse, soon supplanted the H-plan as the basis of the Municipal Building's design.

The final vote gave first place and $1,500 to Long and Kees, second place and $1,000 to W. H. Dennis (Long and Kees' only real competition in the arm-twisting competition), third prize and $600 to Bell (probably a courtesy to William Washburn), fourth prize and $500 to Alexander Murrie, and fifth prize and $400 to G. W. and F. D. Orff (who had the most dramatic renderings). The $3-million-plus "bamboo fishing rod" design beloved by Boyington dropped from the picture entirely.

If there was a sigh of relief in the Long and Kees offices, it was premature. A new fight about what the architects should be paid soon began. The standard fee for public buildings was 5 percent of the cost. But John De Laittre, the strongest friend the chosen architects had on the board, argued strenuously for 4 percent. A compromise was finally reached at 4.5 percent, and this did not change during the two decades of construction.

Finalizing the Plans

With prizes awarded, it remained for the Board of Commissioners to choose the plans it would use. The commissioners had the option of rejecting the prize-winning architect and/or the original plans; that was plain. And exercise the option they did. By the end of June, the Long and Kees open-court and H-plans flip-flopped again. This time, once and for all, the neoclassical palazzo was out; the Romanesque fortress-castle was in.

To assure that Long and Kees would not do a flip-flop with competitors, the architects were asked to amend the Romanesque plan within an even lower budget of $1,150,000. So on July 9, the firm submitted its third set of plans, with the Fifth Street towers reduced from two to one and much of the corner detail and enclosing stone wall eliminated. The main floor was lowered nearly to the Fourth Street level, the foundation was drawn back from the sidewalks, and the open court was expanded to 130 feet square.

This sketch by Long and Kees draftsman A. B. Chamberlin was dated July 12 and appeared in the Minneapolis Journal on July 14. Shortly thereafter it was published in the local Real Estate Review and in the Northwestern Architect. The new plans did not come in under budget guidelines.

These plans finally won over Titus Marek, the last of the H-plan advocates, but they did not come in under budget guidelines. A full story had been added to the Romanesque design entered in the competition, as well as significant ornamentation to the towers and corner pavilions. Long and Kees had hired its own coterie of artist-draftsmen, and the sketch penned by A. B. Chamberlin was more an advertisement for lavish expense than evidence of cost-cutting. To top it off, the Board of Commissioners expressed satisfaction that the plans would last for twenty-five rather than fifty years, at the end of which the city or the county would "give the entire building up to the remaining party."

If there were doubts about how serious the commissioners were regarding the $1,150,000 limit, the next few months removed them. Rather than fine-tune the approved plans—by removing extra rooms, for example—they launched a junket to be sure they and the architects were leaving out nothing of importance. Not satisfied with the twenty-six complete sets of plans available for review—from which the architects were free to borrow—the commissioners took an eastern tour of recently completed civic buildings. Fred Kees was invited, and the group did a fall rail excursion by rail to Chicago, Lansing, Detroit, Indianapolis, Pittsburgh, Philadelphia, Washington, and points between.

The architects then began again. By December 20, the firm was far enough along that the Board of Commissioners took out a building permit. It listed the estimated cost at $2,000,000 and the foundation as a little over 300 feet square, thus taking back the main cost-cutting feature of the July plans. Long and Kees hired Francis W. Fitzpatrick to make a new perspective rendering for publication; it appeared in the *Real Estate Review* concurrent with the permit report.

Long and Kees hired Francis W. Fitzpatrick to draw this perspective of the final plan. It was published with notice of a building permit for $2,000,000.

Working drawings supporting the rendering were at last finished in April 1889, over a year after Long and Kees first submitted plans. Formally approved by the board, the plans became the base for the Municipal Building. The newspapers gave its price as $3,000,000, with much of the interior detailing yet to be determined.

Olaf Hoff designed the steel roof trusses that began to give shape to the Municipal Building in the fall of 1894. On September 21, 1888, H. J. Bauman, the inspector of buildings, had recommended use of "one-half of Fourth street, one-half of Fifth street, one-half of Third avenue and one-quarter of Fourth avenue south on the side next to block 77, town of Minneapolis addition . . . to be used for piling material during the time of construction . . . provided they build a tight board fence seven feet high around the entire block . . . gates to be securely locked at or before sundown of each day, and kept locked during the entire night and Sundays."

Building the Monument

By the time Long and Kees submitted final drawings, a gaping hole already greeted visitors to Block 77. Normally, digging a hole would not make much of a story; but this was the new Municipal Building, and no phase of its construction was without human interest and political intrigue.

Clearing and Excavating

The first job had been to get rid of the existing buildings. Today, when the only required result is rubble fine enough to be trucked away, that stage is handled quickly enough. But in the 1880s, few structures were thrown away, even when they had to give up their sites. With the building boom still peaking and large tracts of near-south Minneapolis still vacant, destroying viable housing made little sense. So the Board of Commissioners sought to sell the properties to anyone who would remove them from the site.

The commissioners did not have long to wait. In June 1888, Charles F. Sawyer came forward with a lump sum of $5,000 for most of the buildings. Sawyer was an attorney then living on the southeast corner of Block 77. His entrepreneurial activities in 1888 evidently propelled him into a new profession, for the 1890 City Directory listed him as a real estate broker. Immediately after purchase, Sawyer carted the old houses on Block 77, one by one, east on Fifth and Sixth streets to new sites. Sawyer's deal with the county ended up being no bargain for the residents along the routes, for many trees were damaged by the houses bumping and jostling down the street. A happier solution emerged for old Washington School: Sawyer took it apart stone by stone, carted the pieces south on Fourth Avenue to Fifteenth Street, and constructed a brick and stone rowhouse, which stood until I-35 plowed through Elliott Park in 1967.

Once the site was cleared, a major obstacle to construction materialized, one proving more political than physical. Two years of agitation by organized

AGREEMENT

Made this 21 day of Dec 1888 by and between the City of Minneapolis, by H. J. BAUMAN Inspector of Buildings, party of the first part, and ~~City Hall & Court House Commission~~ The Court House & City Hall Commissioners part of the second part, that for and in consideration of Building Permit No. A 1180 to them in hand delivered by said party of the first part, said part of the second part agree to do the proposed work in accordance with the description set forth in the application and statement hereto attached, and in the plans and specifications of which the said application and statement are a part, and in strict accordance with the provisions of the ordinance entitled, "AN ORDINANCE TO REGULATE THE CONSTRUCTION, REPAIRS, AND REMOVAL OF BUILDINGS IN THE CITY OF MINNEAPOLIS."

H. J. Bauman (Seal.)

John De Laitre (Seal)

APPLICATION TO BUILD INSIDE FIRE LIMITS.

A1180 Board of Court House & ~~City Hall~~ Commissioners

Owner ~~City Hall & Court House Commission~~

Office of the Inspector of Buildings.

Architect Long & Kees

Builder

Minneapolis, Minn Dec 21 1888

PROPOSED LOCATION OF BUILDING

No.	Street	Part of Lot	Lot	Block	Town, Addition or Subdivision	Ward
4th & 5th St bet 3rd & 4th ave So				77	Minneapolis	5 Plate 29

DESCRIPTION OF BUILDING

Front Width	Depth	Average Height	No. Stories	Built of	Manner of Construction	To be used as	To be Completed	Estimated Cost
307	307	100	5	Stone, Brick & Iron	Fireproof	City Hall & Court House		2,000,000.00

Plumbing permit 7172
" " 22347
" " 18010
" " 10230
" " 15325

I hereby certify that the above statement is substantially correct:

The original permit for construction of the Municipal Building, signed by H. J. Bauman, the inspector of buildings, and John De Laittre, chairman of the construction committee, authorized an expenditure of $2,000,000.

labor had garnered enormous publicity and won some adherents in local government for an eight-hour day and payment by the day rather than by contract. But no major building project had been put up by the day, and the city's business community, led by the Board of Trade, was flat out against either reform.

On July 7, 1888, two days before Long and Kees submitted the third set of plans, the Minneapolis Trades and Labor Assembly convened. Its most important act was to direct a new courthouse committee to "represent to the commissioners that the trades assembly, and the vast majority of working men in the city, were opposed to the contract system, and in favor of day work, and to use their best endeavors to secure the adoption of the day work system."

Thomas H. Lucas was dispatched to the next meeting of the Board of Commissioners, where he made an impassioned plea on behalf of the day labor. The view of organized labor was already represented on the Board of Commissioners by its two strong labor union members from the county board of supervisors, John Swift and Oliver Erickson. City councilmen Lars Swenson and David Clough could also be counted on for support. Swift, Erickson, and Clough were members of the construction committee, so labor was assured a strong voice. But the chairman of the committee, John De Laittre, was opposed to day labor, and most of the remaining commissioners lined up behind him. The main reason was obvious: cost overruns would fall directly in the lap of the commissioners and ultimately on the doorstep of the citizens.

The deadlock in the Board of Commissioners threatened to hamstring construction before the first shovelful of dirt could be removed. But compromise from an unexpected source got the construction process started. Erickson was convinced that the main excavation hole was the wrong place to pitch a tent for the day-labor battle. Picks and shovels could not compete against the steam shovel in handling quantities of dirt, and making the city and county pay for an antiquated means of labor along with hundreds of tools to be used for sixty days only would "give labor a black eye from which it could not recover for many years." So Erickson proposed digging the great hole under contract, with handwork around the perimeter foundation under the day-labor system. After a pitched battle between Swift and De Laittre, who saw no room for compromise, the gist of Erickson's proposal was accepted, with the main excavation contract to be let to the lowest bidder and the remaining work done by day labor "as far as practicable."

The compromise and Sawyer's quick work in removing standing structures from Block 77 enabled the Board of Commissioners to advertise for bids in early July. The final plans would not be in place for nine more months, but at least the length and width of the hole had been determined. By the end of the month, the contract was let to the local firm of Balch and Wetherbee, and the first stages of excavation began.

Two physical hardships soon plagued the excavators. First, more dirt had to be removed from above street grade than below. Both Union School and Washington School had been built on a small knob, 18 feet above the Fourth Street grade. That rise was probably a major reason for the choice of the site in the 1850s. But for the 1880s project, it was a detriment. A building with a 345-foot tower scarcely required a hill to give it prominence; furthermore, with an anticipated volume of 11,000,000 cubic feet, the building needed to run all the way to the sidewalk on four sides.

No local place could receive so much dirt. Excavating had to begin with carting a hill at the heart of the city to a site near its outskirts. The Board of Commissioners let the contractors dump some of the sand on nearby lots for eventual use in mortar and cement, but the contractors paid dearly for that privilege, receiving a lower rate per cubic yard for the materials it dumped in closer areas.

By the end of the summer, Balch and Wetherbee had dug the hole to six feet, all that the plans of July seemed to call for. But the plans evolving out of Kees' inspections of other courthouses brought the Fourth Street entry to street grade. That dropped the basement floor two feet, springing a costly surprise on the contractors. The Board of Commissioners had protected itself against such an eventuality by stipulating in the contract that excavation must be carried to any depth required. This gave the contractor no choice but to continue digging. There was compensation for each cubic yard removed, but the deeper yards cost more in hours. Thus Balch and Wetherbee became the first of many contractors on the building to rue the day it had "won" a work award. And it became living proof of the risks of the contract system, even when the bottom line remained open.

The day-labor forces had a brief moment in the sun when Ring and Tobin was awarded the contract for the foundations of the Fourth Street tower, with the stipulation that all work, as far as practicable, would be done by the day. Ring and Tobin operated a large sandstone quarry near Hinckley, Minnesota, which had recently been opened to massive mining operations. Work on the tower foundations started early in November. On the last day of 1888 the first piece of the building, a massive block of Kettle River sandstone, was placed. It sat directly on the limestone bedrock 34 feet below street grade, in an 18-by-18-

foot pit like the three others anchoring the tower. By the end of winter those four pits were filled, and the tower foundation was complete to the 8-foot level of the general foundation.

Politics Again

In the meantime, the wrangling between day-labor and contract-labor factions on the Board of Commissioners had reached such an impasse that the project was threatened with a shutdown. Temporary solutions like the excavation compromise would plainly not suffice, for the conflict would continue at each stage of bidding. Legislation was the answer. Pro-contract forces, led by the Board of Trade, lobbied in the 1989 session for a bill swelling the Board of Commissioners from nine to twelve and offering as candidates three avowed contract labor men for the new posts.

George A. Brackett

Passage of the bill was a foregone conclusion, for each of the proposed new members had a strong personal and professional profile in the state. Foremost was George A. Brackett, a pioneer businessman who had directed the westward push of the Northern Pacific Railroad from Duluth to the Red River. Brackett went on to serve the city in official capacities, from first chief of the volunteer fire department to mayor to founder of Associated Charities. In addition he had been the unanointed leader of all public celebrations and festivities since the return of soldiers from the Civil War. His enormous popularity and reputation for compassion and fairness gave organized labor a tough opponent.

Edgar F. Comstock was the second new member named in the 1890 bill. A successful building contractor, he was an ideal adversary to the organized labor point of view. His experience also equipped him for chairmanship of the Construction Committee, which fell on his shoulders after De Laittre's resignation in 1896. The third slot was filled by Edward M. Johnson, a distinguished lawyer who had been city council president for many years and succeeded to the presidency of the Board of Commissioners in 1894. The 1910 *History of the Municipal Building* called him the artist and scholar of the board, and he proved himself an eminently capable administrator through years of managing the building process to completion.

Day labor faced its Waterloo on May 22, 1889. On that day, Bengt Aronson's low bid of $131,539 was accepted for the excavation and laying in of the foundation, doing away once and for all with the "day labor so far as practicable" solution. Desperately, Oliver Erickson tried to outflank his growing opposition by pushing for an even lower bid using cheaper material. Only Titus Marek, the chief tightwad of the Board of Commissioners, was won over, and Erickson's constituency on the board deserted him. After a slowdown of nearly half a year and a stoppage of two months, the labor question was resolved and construction began in earnest.

Laying Stone and Throwing Stones

Initial plans for the Municipal Building failed to specify the sort of stone to be used, or even whether the building was to be of stone or brick. All three stages of presentation drawings illustrated a building of stone, with the profusion of carved ornament shown in the "final" working drawings of April 1888 implying a soft or "free" stone. But the matter was left up to the Board of Commissioners, which could be ruled by the architects' recommendations or pursue its own criteria based on appearance, immediate costs, or long-term economies. Three types of stone eventually came into play, each with its own strengths.

The footings were an easy matter. Where the bedrock was out of reach of the foundations, Aronson laid in stone of precisely the same character as the bedrock itself: great slabs of laminated Platteville limestone. This had already been successfully used in nearly all the Twin Cities' building foundations, a practice to continue well into the twentieth century. Possessed of great compression strength but crude appearance, Platteville limestone was also the least-expensive masonry material available. The Board of Commissioners drove the price still lower by contracting directly with the Franklin Cook estate for the stone; that deal was struck over a week before it hired the contractor.

Edward M. Johnson

For the foundation work, local limestone was supplanted by the Kettle River sandstone already used in the great pier foundations of the Fourth Street tower. The architects expressly recommended against using the more convenient Minneapolis stone, on grounds of both cost and durability. For $2,000 more than the estimate on purchasing and laying in local limestone, the Board of Commissioners could get one of the highest grades of sandstone in the country. The state geologist had already proven its compression strength nearly equivalent to that of granite, and sandstone was far easier to dress cleanly than the local limestone. Available in a buff or pinkish hue, it was extraordinarily attractive as a finished surface. For once, the Board of Commissioners yielded to the architects' recommendations without debate, and in May 1889, Kettle River sandstone got the nod.

At this point, it appeared sandstone would not be restricted to the foundation but become the primary material of the superstructure. Ring and Tobin had poured nearly $150,000 into its Hinckley operation in anticipation of contracts like this. Had it gone through to completion, half a million cubic feet of sandstone would have come down the rails to Minneapolis. Then granite came to the fore.

In June 1888, just as the Municipal Building architectural competition was being decided, James Baxter and Son opened a quarry of red granite in Ortonville, clear across the state. That fall, Baxter invited the Board of Commissioners to visit his quarries, which had not yet been worked. But the view of massive outcroppings of the stone and a cut where the granite was twenty feet thick, supplemented by the testimony of the state geologist, N. H. Winchell, assured the board there was plenty of high-quality stone available. To these assurances Baxter added the endorsement of C. W. Hall of the U.S. Geological Survey. Hall particularly recommended the stone for its "bright and cheerful color," its susceptibility to a fine polish, and its occurrence in ledges so free of seams that huge, flawless blocks could be quarried. Though less effusive, Winchell recommended the stone for its "excellent qualities."

Armed with these endorsements, James Baxter and Son had bid on the foundation work for the Fourth Street tower in late 1888. Though the board wisely chose to forego the luxury of granite for stonework that would be buried, its quality was not lost on the commissioners. On July 8, 1889, they formally adopted Ortonville granite as the facing material of the "basement," what is now called the ground floor. The material was to extend to a height of nearly 18 feet, with a further extension to 37 feet for the Fourth Street entry. Kettle River sandstone would remain the material of the inner court, and Bedford stone (a widely used limestone from Indiana) would line the Fourth Street entry. The question of stone for the superstructure above the basement was left open for further discussion.

The contractor for all of this work was C. F. Haglin, one of architect F. B. Long's former partners. His contract for $245,000, including all masonry materials, was far and away the largest paid so far for any building project in the city. It was also the last contract for stonework on the Municipal Building to escape the stone supplier; thereafter, James Baxter and Son and the successor firm, William Baxter, won all the contracts that included use of Ortonville granite.

Titus Marek

During summer of 1890, the basement rose nearly to the height of a two-story building, its massive and colorful facings making a favorable impression on the public. For many of the most vocal admirers, that the remainder of the building might be of any other stone, whatever the cost, seemed unthinkable. One local newspaper ran a series of interviews with prominent citizens who favored the use of hard stone. On the Board of Commissioners they found a ready ally in Titus Marek, a stickler for the more economical H-Plan two years before but also a champion of granite from the outset. Under intense public pressure, the commissioners ran tests on all available materials, including the brownstones of Lake Superior, before their final and complete conversion into "granite men."

Now that the outspoken public had gotten its way, the winds suddenly changed, and another sector of the public raised its voice. No sooner was the word out that the commissioners were leaning toward granite for the entire building than the board was lambasted for extravagance. The long-sleeping truth that estimates of the building cost already exceeded the authorized outlay by more than $1,000,000 suddenly awoke to cries of consternation. In meeting after meeting, the Board of Trade harpooned the Board of Commissioners for its financial irresponsibility and neglect of the public weal. Charles Loring, an original member of the latter board, spoke seriously about tearing the work out and starting over on a less pretentious scale.

In the fall, matters came quickly to a head. On September 13, the Board of Trade called for a report from its committee on public affairs, composed of some of the most highly respected members of the community: John S. Pillsbury, Isaac Atwater, Dorilus Morrison, and F. H. Peavey, among others. After careful review of the plans and a survey of the premises of the new courthouse, the committee concluded that the building was too large and too expensive for the community, that the work be suspended at once, that a new building be planned at one-half the size, and that an injunction be sought if the Board of Commissioners insisted on ignoring the ceiling implied by the $1,500,000 legislative allotment (which included the $321,000 spent on purchasing and clearing the lot).

The Board of Commissioners responded by digging in its heels. At the regular meeting on November 21, Titus Marek moved that granite be formally approved for facing the entire superstructure on the foundation already in place, adding that "a barn-like structure will hardly be a fitting credit to the city of Minneapolis." Only De Laittre voted against the motion. The board thus reiterated its approval of plans to erect a building now estimated at $2,526,000.

According to the *Minneapolis Times,* the commissioners' decision "was received with a howl of derision and bad temper." A chorus of architects, including those who had lost the design competition, echoed the suspicion of the Board of Trade that $4,000,000 was a more accurate figure. It was all to little avail. On December 13, the threatened injunction was requested, on December 20 it was heard by Judge William Lochren, and on December 27 the case was dismissed on the grounds that the authorizing legislation did not limit expenditure to the figure it authorized. It was up to the Board of Commissioners to devise a scheme for raising the rest. This came chiefly in the form of a "county series" of bonds amounting to $1,000,000, approved by the legislature in 1893, and two "city series," approved in 1901 and 1905.

This twenty-three-ton block of granite about to leave Ortonville was one of many bound for the site of the new Municipal Building.

The Board of Trade got in a few last licks, putting off approval of the new county bonds but not affecting the building's design or materials. Costs did not exceed the authorized amount until the end of 1891; by that time the dramatic cornerstone celebration of July 16 had made the finishing of the building according to its original scheme all but inevitable. Yet Isaac Atwater remained resolute: when he assembled his monumental history of Minneapolis and Hennepin County in 1892, he wrote as if granite were confined to the basement.

The one man to profit from the lengthy suits and complaints against the Board of Commissioners was its attorney, Daniel Fish. Though he was paid only a pittance for his enormous efforts on behalf of the board—Fish worked for nothing when the money ran out in 1896—the appointment was the making of his career. No stranger to politics because of his appointment as attorney for the Board of Park Commissioners and the State Park Commission, Fish proved as adept at anticipating and circumventing challenges to the Board of Commissioners' authority as he was at converting judges to its point of view. He played

Embedded beneath the cornerstone in a sealed box of copper were copies of all daily, weekly, and monthly periodicals published in the county; the Minneapolis Journal Souvenir; Minneapolis Illustrated published by the Board of Trade; eighth annual report of the Chamber of Commerce; Hudson's Dictionary of Minneapolis, 1891; Davison's Minneapolis Directory, 1890; city charter, ordinances, and rules in two volumes; proceedings of the Minneapolis City Council, 1890; annual reports of city officers and boards, 1889 and 1890; list of county commissioners; financial statement of Hennepin County, 1890; legislative acts related to the Board of Commissioners and its bylaws; annual reports of the secretary, 1889 and 1890; statement of receipts, expenditures, and liabilities to date; and an invitation to the laying of the cornerstone.

an active role in many of the board's deliberations and proved his familiarity with the history of the Municipal Building's design and execution by finishing and editing the commissioners' final report, issued as a commemorative book in 1910.

While the political titans warred over building materials and costs, the workers waged a lively battle of their own. Some of the soft-stone (sandstone and limestone) cutters were convinced that the labor men on the board were in bed with the hard-stone (granite) cutters. Making matters worse, most of the hard-stone cutters were out-of-towners, employed by the quarry directly and wandering from town to town as the work required. Among the locals, the operant word for a person who did this was *tramp*. The Minneapolis newspapers jumped into the fight, not to take sides but to pick up the choicest invectives for quotation. Apparently words were all that were thrown, for the two groups of stonecutters ended up working amicably together for the duration.

By the time the county side, on the east half of the building, was formally opened in 1895, masonry wall materials including 350,000 cubic feet of granite, over 250,000 cubic feet of sandstone and a similar amount of limestone, some 13,350,000 bricks, and 170,000 square feet of structural partition tile had gone into construction. According to a report of the *Minneapolis Times*, "If the granite had been cut in cubic blocks of one foot, and those blocks were placed in line, they would form a royal road 66 miles in length." The bricks would stretch even further; placed end to end, they would form a line past Portland, Maine, to a point 50 miles at sea.

The Laying of the Cornerstone

During its long construction, the Municipal Building was the site of three public celebrations. The first of these was the laying of the cornerstone, on July 16, 1891. By this time, the Fourth Street side of the building was nearly two stories high by the standards of ordinary construction. As the author of the final report of the Board of Commissioners drolly remarked, "many stones quite as necessary had been long in place." But this 17-foot wall embraced a single story that the upward slope of the street turned into a basement at the point it reached the Fifth Street side. So the cornerstone was laid as expected for datestones, immediately below the basement cap or "watertable."

The corner in question, however, was not the corner of the building but the right end of the projecting entry bay, one of the few parts of the exterior never struck by sunlight. Originally the datestone was intended to terminate a long inscription identifying the city and county sides of the building. A wide course of granite to receive the inscriptions was set in above the arches, but the work never progressed beyond polishing the face of the stones and providing blocks for decorative carving at either end.

Hidden from street view though the cornerstone is, its laying was a great public occasion. A parade escorted by one hundred police patrolmen looped through the downtown from the Masonic Building (also designed by Long and Kees) on Hennepin and Sixth Street down Hennepin to Tenth Street, then over to Nicollet and back up to Fifth, then out Fifth Street to Third Avenue. Several commanderies of the Knights Templar contributed ranks of "sword lines" to the parade. Also featured was the Board of Commissioners and its special guests, members of the Granite Cutters Union. Upon arrival at Third Avenue and Fourth Street, the Grand Masonic Lodge conducted the formal exercises.

Judge Isaac Atwater

By this time the crowd was packing streets, rooftops, and trees. A reporter for the *Minneapolis Tribune* estimated that a hundred people were perched in trees on Fourth Street, and the Third Street lots across the street were filled with women and children, their husbands and older sons occupying the closer spots on the street. Mayor P. B. Winston gave a brief speech in praise of the building and the city, followed by the main oration of the day. Lawyer Frank Davis praised the building of the courthouse as a significant moment in the progress of civilization. Though his speech had overtones of white racial superiority, it was simply one local example of a theory then almost universally accepted in Europe and America. "The progress of architecture," he intoned, "symbolizes the advance of civilization. Where the forest cave, the wigwam of boughs, the tent of skin yield to walls of stone and mortar, there civilization has fixed a sojourning place and created a milestone in its onward march."

The Finishing of the County Side

On November 11, 1895, the county side of the Municipal Building opened to great fanfare, the culmination of two years of extraordinary activity on both the financial and constructive ends. Depletion of the initial appropriation had brought work practically to a standstill in 1892, the year after the laying of the cornerstone. The continued opposition of Judge Atwater and the Board of Trade and a vaguely worded legislative act of 1891 outlawing "special legislation" for local affairs delayed funding efforts until 1893. Even when the "county series" was finally tendered, it was forced to run a gauntlet of legal challenges. The final issuance of the bonds in March 1894 was a personal triumph for attorney Fish as well as further vindication of the board's ambitious undertaking.

The workers must have returned to Block 77 in the spring of 1894 with a tremendous sense of relief. The slowdown of construction had been attended by a severe, nationwide economic depression. Minneapolis building starts had been cut nearly in half between 1892 and 1894. Renewal of Municipal Building construction was thus the 1890s equivalent of a major public works project. Not only was construction under way, but it also was pushed from the top. To ready the county side of the building for occupancy in one year meant work for hundreds of tradesmen, from stonecutters and ironworkers to plasterers, painters, heating contractors, and electricians.

Five county officials gathered at the Fourth Avenue entrance on November 11, 1895, the day the county side of the Municipal Building opened. They were (left to right) commissioners John B. Ryberg, Michael W. Nash, Edward J. Conroy, Albion Barnard, Matthew Walsh, and county auditor Clayton R. Coley.

The county side opening on November 11 was spectacular. That few of the spaces and components being rushed to completion actually made the September deadline was obscured by a spectacular light show sponsored by the Board of Commissioners. Fourth Street from Nicollet Avenue to the building entry was "ablaze with arc lamps strung on wires across the street." One of the merchants hired a band to play under the lights on the sidewalk, and Farmers and Mechanics Bank did the unheard-of, remaining open at night. The lighting extravaganza culminated in the brilliant illumination of the high tower. As the tower had not yet been electrified, the source of the light was five fires, one at each of the four corners and another within the still-vacant clock space. The *Minneapolis Tribune* gushed, "The people of Anoka had no difficulty in seeing where [board president Edward] Johnson was piling on the powder to make the flames redder."

At the site, crowds were treated to an open beer bar "across the way" from the "veritable bower" that the building had become. Floral arrangements occupied every space reasonably protected from the press of the crowds. Twelve thousand people at a time were reported on the first two floors of the county side, with thousands of others mounting the steps to the courtrooms above.

Three parts of the building elicited the most media attention during the frenzied construction of 1894 and 1895: the Fourth Street tower, the Fourth Street entry including the rotunda and elevators, and the county courtrooms. That these were the sites of the most elaborate construction was fitting, for they were also the symbolic essence of the building. The 250,000-ton, 345-foot tower made the building an instant icon of city progress, much like the IDS tower in the 1970s. Not only was it the most visible landmark in the city, but it also offered a view of unexcelled range and sweep. Immediately beneath the tower, the Fourth Street entry ushered all who used it directly into the hub of

The clock tower, a favorite of locals and visitors alike, is prominent in this 1906 view of the Municipal Building from the roof of the Metropolitan Building.

the building. Even in its unfinished state, the rotunda was one of the grandest ceremonial spaces in the city, a five-story court with little practical purpose but access to elevators and stairs. Finally, the courtrooms were the heart of the county side, the locus of justice publicly wielded and gaudily celebrated.

No feature of the building quite caught the public fancy as the main tower did. In addition to it symbolic function, it had four practical uses: to embrace a multistory vault for the auditor and the clerk of courts, to protect a carillon of bells, to hold a giant clock, and to bring visitors of the building to a lookout near the peak of the roof.

The tower vaults, now a restricted-access Municipal Reference Library, posed a unique challenge to the architects in making a narrow vertical space work for the storage and perusal of books. Long and Kees solved the problem by introducing a combination of ornamental bronzed-iron staircases, galleries stacked in vertical succession, and a minuscule elevator shaft. Today, this is the only space in the building that has room for a few things more.

No part of the Municipal Building caught the public fancy quite so much as the main tower, visible from Park Avenue, above.

The last "story" of the tower, immediately above the vaults, was built as a colonnade open on four sides. It was always intended, by architects and commissioners alike, to hold a large bell or bells to sound the time. The carillon of fifteen bells occupying the tower today and ranking among the finest in the country far outstrips their original dreams.

The first act of the Board of Commissioners toward purchase of the "chime of bells" was a well-orchestrated scheme to get the best for the lowest price. On July 25, 1895, the board called in representatives of the Buckeye Bell Company of Cincinnati and the Meneely Bell Company of Troy, New York. Meneely was the oldest and most famous bell manufacturer in the country, and the firm was still in family hands. Fred Kees had stated his preference for hiring the Meneelys outright, and he was strongly supported by the board's president, Edward M. Johnson. Buckeye Bell, though a highly regarded manufacturer as well, was invited (to the firm's chagrin at discovering it) simply to keep the Meneely bid honest. When Meneely came in at 40 cents a pound and Buckeye at 22, Johnson waved the Buckeye figure in front of the Meneely representative and got him down to 35 cents, then to 30 cents. The Board of Commissioners voted to offer him 28 cents, and the deal was closed.

Initially, there was some public pressure to mount a single monster bell, the "largest in the West." Experts advised against this proposition, and two days after the Meneely bid, the board decided to order a "peal" of six bells weighing a total of 22,700 pounds. The cost, including transportation and installation, was set at $6,356. The Board of Commissioners had now succeeded in getting the 28-cent manufacturing figure agreed upon by Meneely to cover delivery and setup costs as well.

To the original peal of six bells, four were added by donation of six Minneapolis citizens, making ten in all and enabling the bell ringer to play in several keys. The donors were men engaged heart and soul in the courthouse work: granite contractor William Baxter, in memory of his recently deceased father, James; architect Fred Kees, in the name of his daughter, Elsa Louise; architect F. B. Long, in the name of his children, who were then draftsmen in his office; Charles Preston, secretary of the board, in the name of his daughter, Sarah; general building contractor C. F. Haglin; and the Fireproof Construction Company, which had manufactured and installed patented fireproofing.

Despite Meneely's reputation, the quality of the bells heard today was a long time in the making. In December 1895 Kees and a committee of experts on bells traveled to Troy at the Meneely brothers' invitation, tested the bells, and found them out of tune and variable in tone. Four days of filing and tests failed to satisfy, so the committee returned to Minneapolis empty-handed. The maker proposed arbitration, but the Board of Commissioners took the hard line that bells that did not chime perfectly were worthless. Finally, after more adjustment and some recasting, the bells arrived in Minneapolis on February

27. An open "bellroom" 25 feet square and about 10 feet high was installed complete with machinery to ring the bells automatically at the quarter-hour. The keyboard to operate the pneumatic system that chimed the bells on special occasions found a place just beneath the bellroom, requiring the ringer to ascend 242 steps (and deafen himself) whenever the city wished to celebrate.

On March 16, all construction was finished, the bells were eased into place between the columns of the gallery, and Chester Meneely launched into a medley of tunes. The sounds of "America," "Home Sweet Home," and "Blue Bells of Scotland" carried clearly as far as the University of Minnesota campus, and all parties were satisfied with the perfection of the tone. The following day the Meneely brothers at last returned home with full pockets.

Inside the tower was a carillon of bells, inspected here in about 1900.

Each of the magnificent new instruments was struck of an alloy comprised of 78 percent copper and 22 percent tin, the standard for high-quality carillon bells. The Meneelys claimed for the carillon "the distinction of being the largest chime of bells in America, if not the world." To this claim the 1910 commemorative *History of the Municipal Building* added: "Whether it has since been excelled in size or weight the writer is not advised, but in purity of tone and carrying power superiority is hardly possible."

The carrying power of the bells was in fact so superior that some citizens complained of being kept awake at night. The largest bell sounded the hour, and a peal of bells set to "Westminster Chimes" announced the quarter-hour. One South Minneapolis resident, Nina Cohen, finally wrote the Board of Commissioners in January 1897. Receiving no action, she initiated a petition signed by Thomas Lowry and others. On hearing the petition, the commissioners instantly acted to eliminate the chiming between 11:00 P.M. and 5:00 A.M.

In 1912, the official bell ringer, Joseph Auld, lodged another complaint: ten bells were inadequate to ring the national anthem. After a ten-year private fund-raising effort spearheaded by Auld, four more bells were purchased from Meneely and installed in 1924. The set of fourteen bells was soon used to raise money for the Minneapolis Symphony Orchestra by chiming out jazz tunes.

Although the tower boasted a carillon of bells and a clock with huge running works (above right about 1900), the crow's nest from which visitors could view the city was its most popular feature. A sketch (above) of a plan for the lookout appeared in the Minneapolis Tribune in November 1895. Below right is Third Avenue, 1908, as seen from the completed tower.

On the same date the Meneely Bell Company was contracted to make and install the first carillon, Johnson Electric Company was awarded the contract for the tower clock, the master clock, and the pneumatic systems connecting them with the bells. Each of the four faces of the tower clock was 24 feet and 8 inches in diameter, making it the largest clock in the world. Its minute hands, cast of solid copper, were 12 feet long, prompting the *Minneapolis Times* to calculate that the tip of each hand would travel 110 miles a year. The frames of the clock faces were of iron, and the expanse of the face within the frame was plate glass half-an-inch thick, permitting illumination from the back.

Despite boasts about outdoing Big Ben in the local newspapers, the dimensions of the clocks were determined purely by architectural considerations. As Kees reported, "the size is exactly in accord with the architectural rule requiring an increase in size of one foot for every 10 feet in height."

Magnificent though the vertical vault, bells, and clock were, the *piece de résistance* of the tower was a cylindrical crow's nest inserted in the peak of the roof. This crow's nest was a dramatic lookout platform from which the citizens

could peer out over Minneapolis from a vantage point 335 feet above the sidewalk. They reached it by a combination of elevator and stairway, the former running through a projecting corner of the tower. Visitors and employees alike navigated the long stretch above the fifth floor up narrow winding steps terminating in a 50-foot open spiral staircase. By 1911, more than a hundred thousand Minneapolitans and visitors a year were ascending the elevator and stairs to the lookout. After World War I, stricter safety standards closed the ascent to all but a few hardy city and county employees, and reroofing of the tower in 1950 sealed off the outlook.

The Fourth Street entry was finished not for the county opening but for the unveiling of the Father of Waters in 1906.

The outfitting of the tower was originally intended as part of the general finish of the Fourth Street entrance, including vestibule, halls, stairs, elevators, and rotunda. But not even the new county bonds could cover it all. Only the triple vestibule, the floor of the rotunda, and the county elevators were completed in time for the opening of the county side on November 11, 1895. The remainder waited for the unveiling of the *Father of Waters,* over ten years later.

Early interior work comprised some of the most unusual aesthetic features of the building. The entire vestibule and rotunda floor were originally covered with mosaic English tile. The architects, supported by Commissioner Brackett, insisted on English tile throughout because of its superior durability, getting their way only in the Fourth Street entry. In the center vestibule, colored pieces of tile forming the state seal were laid in time for the county side opening in 1895. Five years later, a grander representation of the seal of Minneapolis lay in the center of the rotunda floor.

Ironically, most of the interior work given priority for early completion disappeared without a trace in fewer than ten years. These decorated floors were the first to go, for they received too much abuse even for imported tile. The

Fourth Street entrance had been used as a horse stable by the fire department since the early days of construction, and the practice continued through 1904. Furthermore, neither the vestibules nor the rotunda were heated until 1906, when the rotunda was finally finished. By the time the floors were sufficiently protected, they had become a patchwork of tile and cement repairs. In 1906 they were replaced by the stone slabs seen today.

Marble work flanking the three doorways was also replaced in 1906, as it failed to fit the color scheme developed in the rotunda. Only the vaulted Bedford stone ceilings of the three vestibules remain, sole tokens of the 1895 rush to finish the Fourth Street entry.

The fittings of the county auditor's office (below right) were not so elaborate as those of the main courtroom (right). No matter—county officials (far right) were eager to reside in their new quarters anyway.

Within the rotunda, the showiest accomplishment of 1895 was the installation of three ornamental copper elevator cages on the county side. The elevators that ran inside these cages were a different matter; their failure ultimately led to the demise of the cages that contained them. Early in 1895, the Board of

Commissioners chose a barely tried model of electric elevator over the reliable hydraulic type. In addition to their appeal as part of the craze for electric machinery, the elevators selected were less expensive to install and operate. But Kees was dead set against them, and so was the consulting engineer for the Board of Commissioners.

In one of its few acts of incontestably poor judgment, the board ignored its architect, fired the engineer, and chose the Sprague Electric Elevator. When the elevators failed to meet the company's guarantee a year after installation, the issue of paying the contractor arose for deliberation. John De Laittre, who had sided with the architect and engineer, resigned from the Board of Commissioners. Repairs sufficient to the guarantee got the company and the board off the hook in 1897, but the elevators failed to last even until the opening of the city side in 1906. By that time a new Municipal Building Commission had been created to manage the finished parts of the building. It was promptly stuck with the bill for replacement. The original copper cages went to the scrap heap before they could be visually recorded.

The Finishing of the City Side

After the sudden burst of activity to finish the first four floors of the county side, construction slowed until the city could come up with financing for its side. By October 1899, so little had been accomplished on the city side that the board voted not to heat it through the winter. The following year and a half brought little change, though mayor-elect Albert Ames repeatedly pressured the Board of Commissioners to let him move in as early as January 1, 1901. The only highly decorated space ready at that time was the mayor's reception room; his office had yet to be designed.

The raising of a $250,000 bond issue in 1901, followed by an identical authorization four years later, finally led to the city side's completion. The first flurry of construction began in mid-1901 and culminated in a formal opening on December 16, 1902. At that time, the city half, including the very lavishly appointed city council chambers and park board meeting room, was nearly completed through the fourth floor.

The opening of the city side of the Municipal Building was a relatively calm affair despite a more extensive illumination of Minneapolis than at the county-side opening and the stationing of a large orchestra on one of the landings in the middle of the building. A month's delay in the ceremonies, attended

The city council chambers were elaborate in design and decoration.

by newspaper reports of every detail of the interior, had likely dulled the public appetite. This time the press tempered its tone of unbridled boosterism. Headlines such as "Aldermen Possess Costly Furniture and Assemble in an Ornate Chamber" cut two ways in a city struggling to emerge from the economic doldrums of the 1890s. Moreover, the acoustics of the new council chamber were pronounced atrocious by the aldermen themselves during their first group visit on November 21. As the *Minneapolis Journal* reported, "At first glance the eye is dazzled by the brightness and colors so artistically blended, but when the echoes begin, the auditory nerves are rasped and harried to distraction."

A second flurry of activity, beginning in mid-1905, brought the Fourth Street entry nearly to completion for the unveiling of the *Father of Waters* on August 11, 1906. After many years of planning and replanning, the magnificent Fourth Street entry was opened to public inspection at the unveiling of the sculpture. Providing a suitable setting for the *Father of Waters* accomplished in two years what continuous pressure from the architects and the public had not accomplished in ten.

Rushed to completion for the 1906 unveiling, the central courtyard did not receive much special press coverage. In the original drawings, the architects visualized a circular one-story public lavatory at the base of this great open space in the center of the building. Though eccentric, the plan would put rest rooms in an otherwise dead space and keep them from obtruding into the valuable office space of the first floor. Moreover, in maintaining a one-story height and circular floor plan, the facility would not block light from any of the rooms with windows on the court.

A 50-foot circular enclosure was initiated during the early stages of Municipal Building construction, but it failed to progress beyond a blank brick exterior. For fifteen years the flat cylinder sat in the 130-foot square like a giant round of cheese, inspiring countless architectural fantasies among those who gazed on it from the windows above.

The first inspiration to get newspaper ink came from the park board. In August 1901 its secretary J. A. Ridgway suggested a public year-round bathhouse or, in today's terms, an indoor swimming pool. The connecting rooms on the county side would provide dressing rooms and showers. Prominent architect and fellow park commissioner Harry Jones supported Ridgway's proposal, but it failed to catch on with Hennepin County officials, who would have to supply the funds. Furthermore, the architect, F. B. Long, was incensed at the idea, calling it a "perversion of the original plans."

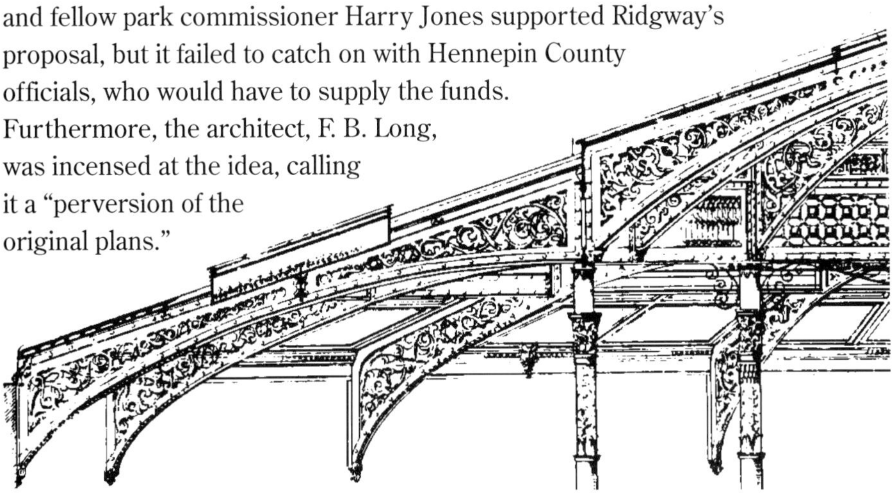

The architects conceived design details such as wrought-iron trusswork as part of a public lavatory scheme for the rotunda.

The next proposal came in 1902 from the Board of Commissioners president, Edward Johnson. After hearing Long give estimates for completion of the building, Johnson pushed for finishing the circular enclosure, which Long had left out of his estimates. Johnson's pet idea was a free reading room, to be operated as a downtown branch of the public library on Hennepin and Tenth. For awhile it looked as if Johnson's proposal might be joined to the original architects' intent, for the *Minneapolis Journal* reported on August 20, 1903, that the circular court would be a branch library, "equipped as a reading room [with] public comfort stations." The proposal died on the vine for lack of Hennepin County support.

In the meantime, a proposal to move the enclosure in the courtyard just a notch toward its "final" disposition had surfaced. In early 1903, a member of the Minneapolis Philharmonic Club suggested an auditorium or general assembly room analogous to the town halls of New England. This time, the idea gathered support in the right places, for in April he was joined by the Minneapolis Real Estate Board, the Minneapolis Retailers Association, and the Minneapolis Commercial Club in appealing to the Board of Commissioners for conversion of the courtyard to an assembly hall. Three days later, a joint delegation of state legislators from Hennepin County announced it was amending the appropriation bill before the legislature so that up to $100,000 could be used for it.

By this time, the architects had begun to see the light: monumental public lavatories did not stimulate appropriations. But they estimated that the 3,000-seat assembly hall envisioned by Hennepin County would cost 50 percent more than the legislators had projected. The point became moot when the 1903 legislature failed to authorize any part of the total bonding of $500,000 sought by the Hennepin delegation. Again, disposition of the interior court went on hold.

In 1905, the Minneapolis post of the Grand Army of the Republic (GAR) stepped in as the champion of the courtyard completion. What it wanted was a scaled-back version of the assembly hall for use in its major meetings or encampments, along with two smaller halls, one for their regular use and the other for the use of auxiliary women's groups. The larger hall would seat around 500 people, the smaller between 75 and 150. When a $250,000 bond issue was approved by the legislature, the Board of Commissioners speedily granted the GAR request, and replanning of the courtyard began in earnest.

The Minneapolis Journal ran this cartoon on August 17, 1895, with a caption reading: "Two Views of the Courthouse Commissioner—As Seen by Himself and as Seen from the Top of the Tower."

The spaces that ultimately took shape within the courtyard were directly in line with the GAR request. After firing the imaginations of so many would-be architects, the above-grade part of the flattened brick cylinder was removed and the courtyard filled with meeting halls and anterooms. The largest hall was designed for conventions and meetings, with the stipulation that the GAR had first use during its major encampments. Construction and outfitting were nearly complete for the GAR reunion encampment the following August, just a couple of weeks before the unveiling of the *Father of Waters.* Basic costs ran around $50,000, or one-third the estimate for the 3,000-seat assembly hall envisioned in 1903.

The End of an Era

Midway through work on the city side, another political body was created to oversee the building as it reached completion. Starting in January 1904, maintenance and control of all finished portions of the building officially passed out of the hands of the Board of Court House and City Hall Commissioners and into the hands of the Municipal Building Commission (MBC). Created by a legislative act on April 18, 1903, its members were the chairman of the board of county commissioners to serve as president, the mayor of Minneapolis to serve as vice president, the county auditor, and the city treasurer. (In 1977 a legislative act amended the law replacing the auditor and treasurer with one appointee of the board of county commissioners and one of the city council.)

During the MBC's first years of operation, skirmishes over turf between the two groups responsible for the building were inevitable. The Board of Commissioners was unwilling to relinquish control of spaces not quite finished but in use, but it was only too willing to let go of spaces finished but in need of repair. The many unassigned rooms, in the meantime, fell between the cracks. Though technically the building was in the control of the Municipal Building Commission, potential commercial tenants continued to apply to the Board of Commissioners.

The Women's Relief Corps occupied the quarters at left in 1907.

On its way to completion, the Municipal Building offered unique opportunity for no-frills temporary spaces to a bizarre mix of tenants. For ten years the tenants came and went, until the Municipal Building passed fully into city and county hands. More than transients, they were also reminders of the rural and small town way of life whose demise the Municipal Building symbolized. They were also a means of offsetting recurrent public resentment over the excesses of the building, particularly its size.

Early occupants included a blacksmith shop adjoining the stable on the ground floor, a chicken hatchery on the second floor, and a wool brokerage on the third floor. During the long period in which they were accessible but unfinished, the city-side rooms also provided temporary quarters for anyone who wanted to convene, exhibit, or put on a benefit. The Minneapolis Outing Association headquartered in the building in the summer of 1896. In 1899, at least three groups leased temporary spaces: the Northwest Kennel Club held a bench show on the first floor, a Labor and Industry Exposition was put on in an unspecified unfinished space, and the schoolchildren of Minneapolis exhibited their drawing achievements on the second floor. Two years later, Asbury Methodist Hospital and the Catholic Orphan Asylum held benefit fairs on the fourth floor of the county side and the drill room next to the city police offices, and in 1902 the Northwest Photographers Association used several city-side rooms for its annual meetings. The Minnesota Poultry Association exhibited on the fourth floor in 1904 and again in 1905. Called the "Chicken Association" by some members of the MBC, the organization was not a popular tenant, though its presence was natural given the long-term lease of the hatchery.

Many of these activities continued well past the nominal completion of construction in 1906, for much of the fourth and fifth floors remained unassigned until courtroom, jail, and office expansions in the 1910s. But their day was short-lived. The completion of the Fourth Street entry set a new tone of seriousness; the building by 1906 had evolved from a symbol of urban life being born to a seat of urban culture being realized.

The ground floor of the rotunda is a showplace for the vision and workmanship of the Municipal Building's designers and artisans. The sculpted Father of Waters and massive light standards stand out against a background of marble and stained glass.

Architects, Artists, and Artisans

The Municipal Building that finally opened to full use in 1906 was the joint product of scores of minds and hands. In the background loomed the great H. H. Richardson, whose Allegheny County Courthouse (see page 14) was the chief inspiration of the building in detail as well as general form. In the foreground center were the architects, Long and Kees. And alongside the architects were dozens of talented draftsmen and designers, many of them anonymous, as well as all the decorators and artisans and manufacturers who had a hand in determining the shape of the final product.

The Architects

Of the partners Long and Kees, Frederick Kees was plainly in charge of the Municipal Building project from the outset. Until the late 1890s, the minutes of the Board of Commissioners referred frequently to him but never to Long alone. Kees' primacy may have been a matter of politics as much as an internal decision of the firm. He had from the start the strongest of backers in John De Laittre, chairman of the construction committee, who knew Kees' work firsthand from his first major local project, the Syndicate Block of 1882.

Kees, known familiarly and professionally as Fred Kees, began his career in the standard way, as a draftsman trained in a succession of architectural offices before setting up business for himself. Born in Baltimore, Maryland, in 1852, he began work at the age of thirteen for architect E. G. Lind of Baltimore. Except for a short break during which he moved to Chicago to work under an obscure architect named T. V. Wadskier, Kees continued to apprentice under Lind until 1878. At that time, he joined the westward immigration of young architects and moved to the Twin Cities.

Like many other architectural trainees from the East, Kees found immediate work in the offices of pioneer St. Paul architect Abraham Radcliffe, whose extraordinarily prolific practice was just starting to wind down, and Minneapolis architect L. S. Buffington, whose career was just beginning to take off. By 1881, Kees apparently was doing well enough to marry another transplanted easterner, Florence Smith, and strike out on his own with Burnham W. Fisk, a fellow apprentice from Buffington's office.

Once in business for himself, Kees' success was instantaneous. During their first year, he and Fisk won a prestigious and hugely profitable competition for a 300-foot commercial building on Nicollet between Fifth and Sixth streets. Dubbed the Syndicate Block because of its backing by a local corporation of fifteen investors, this mammoth structure was heralded by civic boosters as "the largest business block under one roof in America." However inflated these claims may have been, they indicated the magnitude of the accomplishment to the businessmen of the city. From Kees' standpoint the project paid his efforts many times over, for one of those businessmen was John De Laittre, secretary and treasurer for the incorporators.

Fred Kees

Faced with Ohio sandstone and ornamented in a mix of Gothic and Italian Renaissance styles, the Syndicate Block also earned Kees an early reputation as an artist among architects. Whatever role his early partner may have had, Kees' name alone became attached to this triumph. His reputation was further enhanced by the instant remodeling of part of the Syndicate Block into a Grand Opera House in 1883 and his winning of the First Baptist Church commission in the following year. As a result of these monumental commissions alone—and there were many residential triumphs to accompany them—Kees' future was absolutely assured by the time the building boom of the mid-1880s set in.

Kees' domination of the planning and designing process ceased in the late 1890s. For reasons never made publicly plain, Long and Kees parted in 1897, and from that year forward, Long and his successors took over all remaining architectural work, including several early remodelings in the 1910s. Kees was still in the wings, however, and he occasionally stepped in when Long's ever-unpredictable health kept him from performing his duties.

Franklin Bidwell Long had held a place among Minneapolis architects considerably longer than Kees, but his star rose about the same time. Born in South Bainbridge, New York, in 1842, F. B. Long showed an early aptitude for mathematics and mechanical studies. Shortly after his family moved to Illinois in 1859, Long established himself in Chicago as a carpenter and builder. After eight years of practicing the trade, he shifted to architecture, beginning in the offices of the prominent Chicago architect John C. Cochrane; a year later he entered practice for himself with a fellow draftsman from Cochrane's office.

In 1868, poor health drove Long to Minneapolis, where the cold, crisp air was widely believed to be curative. The following year he returned briefly to his home state to marry Gertrude Landers. However healthful the Minneapolis climate might have been, it was not a good time for an architect to begin a career in a fledgling city. After a few years of wildly optimistic real estate speculation, Minneapolis joined the rest of the country in a severe economic depression.

Long was on the verge of returning to Chicago for want of work or even its prospect when he landed one of the few lucrative commissions of 1873, the old Minneapolis City Hall on Bridge Square. This one commission could easily have propelled Long into the front rank of the city's young coterie of architects.

But ill health and a restless spirit plagued him, and he began to dabble in real estate, took on a succession of architectural partners, and spent the late 1870s as chief architect for the west branch of the Milwaukee Road.

Long's career took a decisive turn in 1881, just when Kees was beginning his career as a full-fledged architect. Long had returned to independent practice and begun to invest heavily in local real estate the year before. The first major product of his investments—and his renewed architectural energies—was the Kasota Block, a massive speculative commercial building on the north side of lower Hennepin Avenue whose craggy, unadorned walls were a perfect counterpoint to the urbane air and busy surfaces of the nearly contemporary Syndicate Block. The first commercial building in the state designed in the Richardsonian style, the Kasota Block fixed Long's local reputation as an architect who, above all, knew how to build soundly, whatever the difficulties of the site or demands of the materials.

F. B. Long

In early 1885, when Kees' and Long's separate architectural offices were on a wild upswing, the two joined. The partnership was a perfect fit. Each knew all sides of architectural practice, but each also knew where best to spend his energies. On engineering matters, the two were of equal competence. But though Kees had an unusual facility for facts and figures, he had little patience for the nitty-gritty of mechanical systems and everyday office procedure. At the same time, though Long's independent projects indicated a sure artistic eye, he had come to rely on the services of a master designer and in fact had developed a facility for surrounding himself with top-notch draftsmen.

The two personalities also complemented each other well. Kees was the more gregarious, genial in disposition and popular socially. Long was all business, the picture of the straightforward, resolute man of affairs. "The longer I live," he said, "the more I am certain that the great difference between men, between the feeble and the powerful, the great and the insignificant, is energy, invincible determination, a purpose once fixed, and then death or victory."

Long and Kees were just beginning a fourth year in business together when they submitted their entry to the Municipal Building competition. What they had accomplished in those three years was staggering. In the summer of 1885, their first season of architectural practice together, they won a prestigious local competition for the Masonic Temple on Hennepin and Sixth (now the Hennepin Center for the Arts). The following spring they won the competition for the Minneapolis Public Library building on Hennepin and Tenth (now demolished).

Business savvy had as much to do with the latter commission as architectural know-how, for Long and Kees had been the only architectural firm to subscribe ($3,000) to thc building fund thc year before. By the end of 1886, Long and Kees had also secured the commission for the city's first ten-story building, the Lumber Exchange at Fifth and Hennepin, and construction was under way on its five-story Corn Exchange as well. A year later, these projects were joined by a mammoth retail store for William Donaldson. So by the time the Municipal Building competition circular was released in November 1887, Long and Kees had five major downtown commissions under its belt, all at varying stages of completion. No one could question the firm's competence in handling the largest building projects the city had to offer.

The Draftsmen

With so many projects on the drawing board, Long and Kees found they had to rely heavily on a growing corps of draftsmen for much of their building design work. Though Long and Kees are constantly mentioned in contemporary newspaper accounts and even public speeches, the names of the draftsmen who did the day-to-day work never found their way into print. Yet these draftsmen were more than pencil-pushers. In a project of this magnitude, the principal architects could often function as little more than guides and supervisors once the layout and general forms of the building were settled. This was particularly true for the detailing, ornamentation, and outfitting of the building. H. H. Richardson's famed Boston office is a well-documented case in point. The overall design of the Allegheny County Courthouse was Richardson's own; but the ornamental carving came largely from the minds and hands of apprentices, including student interns from the Massachusetts Institute of Technology.

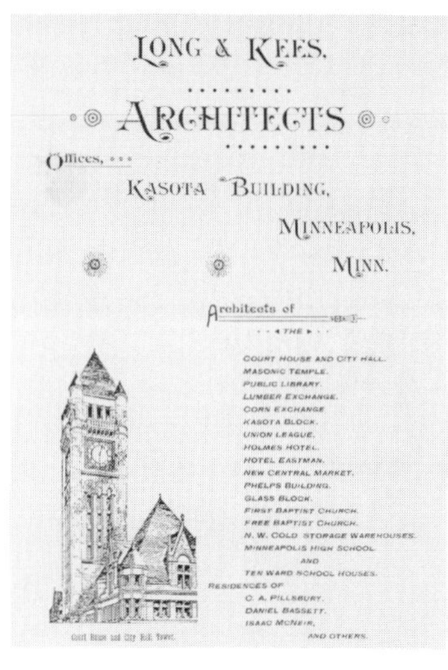

In a practice as prolific as that of Long and Kees, the case could hardly have been any different. As it happens, at the initiation of its Municipal Building design commission, the firm had at least two draftsmen-designers of extraordinary ability and several others available on a free-lance basis. The first of the former group was Arthur Bishop Chamberlin, whom Long had brought over from his independent practice. Chamberlin had come to Minneapolis from Ohio in 1882. Only seventeen at the time and without earlier architectural experience, he likely started at the bottom in Long's expanding Minneapolis office; that usually meant as an office boy. But by April of 1887, when he was still only twenty-two, his skills had propelled him to the position of chief of the Long and Kees office.

Chamberlin's only demonstrable role in the Municipal Building project was in the intermediate design stage expressed by the July 1888 rendering (see page 26) that bears his initials. This rendering shows the simplification of the overall exterior design in the half-year from when the original sketches were submitted, in particular the elimination of gratuitous detail on the corner pavilions and the focusing of ornament onto three main locations: the entry, the dormers, and the area surrounding the clockface. Though much of the ornament, in particular the design of the main (clock) tower, continued to undergo design changes, these advances in the design stuck. The publication of the drawing over Chamberlin's monogram squares with his predilection as a mature designer for complex geometries and restricted ornamentation zones as means of creating dramatic effects. These elements of his architectural persona did not come fully to light until Chamberlin went west in the wake of the Seattle fire of 1889; but their germ was present in the 1887 sketch for Long and Kees. Much of the exuberant carved work originally planned for the Fourth Street entry and tower may also have been his creation.

The month after Chamberlin was appointed office chief, Long and Kees hired Ernest F. Guilbert, another young man with enormous artistic facility. Guilbert had worked for Kees and Fisk in the early 1880s, then wandered the Upper Midwest as a free-lance architectural draftsman-designer. When Kees succeeded in rehiring him in 1887, the local architectural press heralded it as a coup for the firm, for by that time Guilbert was regarded as "one of the leading draftsmen in the city." He immediately applied his considerable and distinctive skills to several Romanesque designs the Long and Kees firm was developing concurrent with the Municipal Building. Locally, the most outstanding example was the new Washington School, built at Sixth Street and Eighth Avenue South (now Chicago Avenue) to replace the building dismantled by C. F. Sawyer on the Municipal Building lot. Guilbert's tenure was, like Chamberlin's, short-lived, for he left Minneapolis again in the early 1890s to become a leading designer for prominent Chicago architect Henry Ives Cobb.

The wandering careers of these two draftsmen were typical of the day. The most talented designer-draftsmen tended to remain single through their youths, living in perpetual motion among the architectural offices of various cities and states. They went where the large projects or expanding prospects were. The Minnesota Architectural Sketch Club was the social and artistic center of their activities in Minneapolis and St. Paul. Established on a formal basis in 1888, it gravitated around the personality and talent of Harvey Ellis.

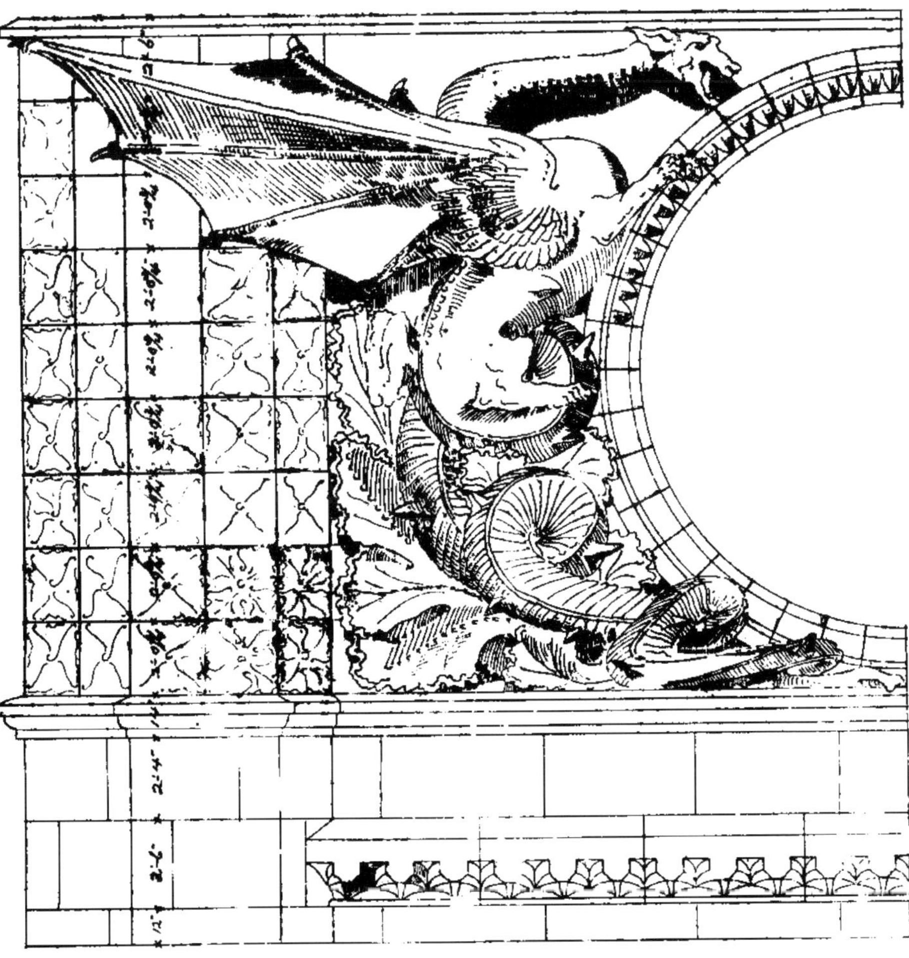

This sketchwork for the stone carving originally planned around the Fourth Street clock (left) may have been the work of draftsman Arthur Bishop Chamberlin.

Ellis was the only one of these nomadic designer-draftsmen to establish an independent reputation carried through to the present day. Such a romance has gathered about him that the usual distribution of credit has been turned on its head, with accomplishments of his employer firms all but lost sight of for the attention paid to this gloriously talented draftsman.

The effect on the architecture of the Upper Midwest of the extraordinary fraternity of nomadic draftsmen that Ellis represented was considerable. These men brought the latest ideas into established architectural offices; and they were responsible for most of the ornamentation of executed buildings, even those of renowned architects.

In the Twin Cities, the force of Ellis' talent and personality was reflected everywhere his colleagues went. Specifically, the draftsman associated with Long or Kees in the 1880s were conspicuously affected by Ellis' distinctive style. E. E. Joralemon, Long's partner in 1880 and again in 1884, Fred Fitzpatrick, who executed the published renderings of the final Municipal Building design, and Chamberlin and Guilbert all were able but rather uninspired renderers before they met Ellis. But around 1887, each radically changed his drawing style to incorporate the humanistic tone, picturesque settings, and eccentric perspectives that gave Ellis' work such strong character. In late 1888, Chamberlin became secretary of the Minnesota Sketch Club, which Ellis led, and the 1887 rendering of the Municipal Building shows that he was touched by the Ellis influence well before that formal connection. Chamberlin and Guilbert may have been joined as required by Joralemon and Fitzpatrick, who were free-lancing during the critical stages of Municipal Building design.

Scarcely twenty years after Louis Long's Gothic design for the city council chambers ceiling was installed, the ceiling was lowered and simplified to correct the acoustics.

With the initiation of work on the interiors of the Municipal Building in the mid-1890s, another group of designer-draftsmen entered the picture. Most prominent among these was F. B. Long's son, Louis, whose Ellis-like renderings of the firm's projects were already finding their way into national publications. By the time the city-side interiors came up for design, H. H. Richardson's bold, medieval-based ornamental style had fallen from favor, and the more delicate lines of the French Renaissance had largely taken its place. Louis Long had in the meantime acquired enough experience in Long and Kees' office to be entrusted with some of the decoration in the new fashion. In an exceptional gesture of recognition to a junior partner—which he had become by 1901—the

Minneapolis Sunday Times credited the florid design of the vaulting in the city council chambers to Louis Long in 1902. This room was for many years one of the most sumptuously appointed interiors in Minneapolis, a bragging place for the locals and a gawking place for the visitors as well as the city's central arena for civic debate and decision-making.

No other names from the Long and Kees office can definitely be linked to the Municipal Building design, though an intriguing inscription on one of the carillon bells reads: "Presented by Mr. Louis L. Long and Miss Jessie Long who have assisted in the erection of this building by preparing the architectural drawings in the office of Long and Kees, Architects, Minneapolis, A.D. 1895." In what capacity and for how Long's daughter worked for the firm has not been determined.

Interior Designers and Decorators

In 1889 and again between 1894 and 1895, Long and Kees prepared a set of plans detailing the interior spaces of the Municipal Building. Some of these, most notably the main courtroom, the Fifth Street lobby, and the mayor's reception room, were completed in close accord with the architects' plans. Others required substantial redesign to accommodate a shift in taste at the turn of the century. But in all cases, the interior decorators hired to execute the design enjoyed a significant degree of latitude.

Lawrence A. McIvor

Lawrence A. McIvor was the first interior decorator to leave his mark on the Municipal Building. Born in Hamilton, Ontario, in 1843, McIvor entered the New York City decorating and furnishing house of Perry and Jackson in 1876. A few years later he formed a partnership in Elmira, New York, with architect Warren H. Hayes. Soon to emigrate to Minneapolis, Hayes became the most prolific church designer in the Upper Midwest. McIvor followed Hayes to Minneapolis in 1888 and, like Hayes, he enjoyed instant success. According to a biography written shortly after his death, "his ability was immediately recognized by architects among whom he was regarded as a man of genius." Long and Kees may have been the first to see a good thing, for the firm immediately put this "artist-decorator" from the East to work on the grand hall and vestibule of the half-finished Masonic Building. The firm drew on his services again for the decorating of the men's and women's reading rooms of the new public library, the sanctuary of the Free Will Baptist Church on Nicollet, and other local projects.

In 1893, McIvor initiated the first of several contracts for the interiors of the Municipal Building. He began in a small way, with decorating the meeting room of the county commissioners. His diminutive fee ($190) indicates that the decorating was not extensive, though the money obviously bought much more that it could buy today (the painter bid $41 for his services). The small commission was in keeping with the times, for the Municipal Building project was stalled between major funding appropriations. Still, the room required enough artistry for the architects to separate it from other spaces on the first floor. Two years later, McIvor received the commissions that gave him recognition far beyond the local circle of architects and contractors: the decorating of eight district courtrooms on the second and third floors of the county side of the Municipal Building. The main courtroom, on the Fourth Avenue side of the third floor, was bid out first, as it was the largest and most elaborate of the eight. McIvor's bid of $600 was accepted on May 7, 1895, with $200 added at the following meeting to honor his wish to use gold leaf rather than bronze paint. On June 25, McIvor's bid of $1,200 for the remaining seven courtrooms was also accepted. Four months later, all of the work was completed, and the county side was ready for public inspection.

The chandeliers shown in early courtroom photographs (see page 44) are not shown in draftsman Louis Long's office sketch (right) of McIvor's design, possibly because they would have obscured the fine detailing of the walls. Their design, however, was unique to the building and quite likely emanated from his studio as well.

When November 9, 1895, arrived and the press got its first glimpse of McIvor's handiwork, the *Minneapolis Sunday Times* declared the main courtroom "the bright particular feature of the new building." It boasted a ceiling of heavy crossing beams and eleven-foot plaster panels, five arched windows running nearly floor to ceiling with a matched blind arcade on the opposite wall, and six-foot paneled wainscoting. Ceiling panels and beams, column capitals, the area around the arches, and the seven chandeliers were all exquisitely cast and molded in the Romanesque manner; other areas of the wall received a multicolored frescoing of arabesques. The prevailing color scheme of green and terra cotta continued into the lesser courtrooms, though their ornamentation was considerably scaled down.

McIvor's role in the design of these interiors was to invent an ornamental scheme compatible with the overall intent of the architects. Long and Kees most likely supplied drawings fixing the style and location of ornament, but it was up to the decorator to develop the detailed drawings, choose the colors, and oversee their execution. In McIvor's case, the decorator probably also worked as the chief artisan in executing the designs, at least for the fresco work and molded plastering.

Though McIvor got the contract for the fanciest work in the courthouse, he lost the much larger commission for all the other walls and ceilings. The local firm of Wagner and Nelson underbid him by 25 percent and got the job. This was typical of the commissioners' handling of the bidding process: whenever highly developed skills or artistry were demanded, the bid was split, with the most qualified artisan or company getting the tough work and the low bidder getting the rest. This procedure, though it may have been cost-effective, pleased nobody: the artisans were irritated at being denied the option to handle the most profitable part of the job along with that yielding greater artistic reward, and the financial watchdogs were irritated because high bidders always seemed to get a foot in the door.

In 1896, McIvor won his fourth commission for a Municipal Building interior, this time a $995 contract for the walls and ceilings of the Fifth Street entrance and lobby. Once again, most of his attention was devoted to the designing and molding of ornamental plasterwork. The ceilings received elaborate Romanesque panels similar to those in the main courtroom, and each of the three monumental entries was set within a double arch of acanthus leaves. The capitals of the piers, adorned with acanthus leaves, extended around the entire vestibule lobby as a wainscot cap. The wainscot of Lisbon marble had been laid in the previous winter at a cost exceeding $20,000. By the time the work was

McIvor designed the ornamental plasterwork of the Fifth Street vestibule, shown at left in 1907.

finished, the molded plasterwork of McIvor was hardly distinguishable from the carved work of the marble-setters.

McIvor's last Municipal Building contract was for the walls and ceilings of the mayor's reception room, executed in the summer of 1900. The first of the city-side rooms to receive its finish treatment, this space offered an upscale variation of the plaster ceiling panel motifs and high wainscoting of the main courtroom. This time the ceiling panels were divided into subpanels, creating a grid-within-a-grid of Romanesque leaves and flourishes. A trifle was saved by substituting mahogany for rosewood wainscoting, but these savings disappeared when the wainscoting was raised to eight and one-half feet. Once again, ceiling and walls were painted in an olive green, tipped with gold leaf, and the wainscoting was stained a deep red; these were complemented by a cream-colored floor of mosaic tile. A *Minneapolis Journal* writer joked that the result would make St. Paul "pea green with envy and yellow with wonder." The journalist continued that, "this room will be one of the showplaces of the city, especially for the rural visitors. It will be strictly ornamental and doubtless of little use, but it will be a beautiful sample of the decorator's art."

McIvor's plan for the mayor's reception room was "a beautiful sample of the decorator's art." The furniture was added later by Boutell Brothers.

Of the five lavish interiors by McIvor, only the Fifth Street lobby is reasonably intact and exposed to view. Although altered in recent years to accommodate an underground connection to the Hennepin County Government Center, the lobby contains the only elaborate decor of the pre-1905 building still visible. What remains of the others has been walled over or hidden behind dropped ceilings. It is also the only remaining example of McIvor's extensive and renowned work for Long and Kees and may well be the sole important survivor of his extensive work in the state.

McIvor's interiors were the only lavish spaces apart from the rotunda to be decorated according to the architects' original concept. In retrospect, that the Romanesque style and the dense green and red color scheme that went with it held on so long is amazing. By 1901, when the last of McIvor's interiors was finished, the Richardsonian Romanesque fad in public building had been dead for nearly a decade. But the architects and interior decorators caught up in a hurry; by 1902, every new interior displayed not the slightest hint of the solemn medieval styling that infused McIvor's work. With a change in tastes, McIvor lost his hold on the plum decoration contracts. Bidding had nothing to do with it. The new interior decoration contracts played against McIvor's strengths, for the ornamental plasterwork in the ceilings was finished by others before the contracts were let. Furthermore, his reputation had attached to his consummate handling of the architects' concepts; now the board was looking for new effects, even if it meant straying from the architects' proposals.

The decorator of the moment was John S. Bradstreet, a prominent member of the city's park board and vice-president of the new Municipal Art Commission, as well as McIvor's only real rival in the city. Bradstreet was an 1874 emigré of New England. Raised by a well-to-do Massachusetts family descended from Pilgrim stock, he was educated at Putnam Academy and trained in the prominent decorating studios of the Gorham Company in Providence, Rhode Island. Bradstreet's Minneapolis business went back and forth between partnerships and sole proprietorships. He was always known as the artist of the firm, his reputation enhanced by several trips to Japan and the development of an international spectrum of designing styles.

John S. Bradstreet

Bradstreet's political connections plainly gave him a foot up on competitors, particularly since the rooms of the park board comprised one of the two elaborate interiors slated for completion in 1902. The other complex decorating job was for the city council chambers. On this commission, McIvor's and Bradstreet's bids were nearly equivalent, but Bradstreet cagily coupled his bid with an offer to reject the historical sketches and start fresh for an additional $125. A week after the proposals had been offered, he pocketed both commissions.

The first of the 1902 contracts finished was the two-story meeting room of the city park board on the third floor. No pictures survive in public collections of this sumptuous interior, unique in the Municipal Building for decoration in the Arts and Crafts manner with a topical theme. A five-foot frieze carrying a fresco of Minnesota birds and foliage ran around the two interior walls of the room, and these motifs were worked out again in the semicircular transoms of each of the tall windows opening onto the Fifth Street and Third Avenue corner. Remaining wall space was colored in the latest shade of green, a subtle tone called "Grueby green," after a fashionable art potter in Boston. Woodwork was of oak treated in the "Japanese" fashion, which meant a weathered look induced by treatment with alkalis and ammonia. Woodwork, walls, and windows were a far cry from the dignified paneled squares and solemn acanthus patterns of the courtrooms and halls finished by McIvor.

For the city council chambers, Bradstreet combined with the architects to design the gaudiest interior of the building. Louis Long had already designed an exuberant filigree of plaster along the ribs of the Gothic ceiling vaults, and to this Bradstreet added a sequence of matched plaster wall panels beneath the transom and balcony arches and two equally embellished transom windows above the doors. The walls and ceilings were painted mandarin blue touched with gold, and the pilasters and vault ribs were painted in imitation of "old metal." All of the furniture was of solid mahogany, and $600 worth of drapes adorned the giant arched windows. Eight chandeliers designed in the most

Bradstreet's scenic painting—Old Government Mill at St. Anthony Falls —was one of two panels executed for the city council chambers (shown in place in altered form on page 56.)

outlandish rococo manner were hung from the pendants of the vault ribs; of solid brass, these fixtures carried 120 globes among them and cost an unheard-of $250 apiece.

Even this did not satisfy all of the city council. On his first viewing of the room, Alderman Lars Rand protested that the windows showed too much bare glass for so ornate a chamber, so the opening of the space to the public was deferred from November to December, and Bradstreet was hired to come up with a floral design for painting on the plate glass in imitation of plaster filigree elsewhere in the room. The most elaborate of these windows was immediately and appropriately dubbed "Alderman Rand's window." Ironically, this last touch was also the first to disappear from the room, for the heat from a fire in a building across the street on November 21, 1903, ruined the painted windows, leading to their replacement by plate glass less than a year after installation.

In 1905, three years after the room was "finished," Bradstreet returned with one last touch: the scenic painting of the plaster panels at either end of the wall opening onto the corridor. For one of these panels, Bradstreet gave the obligatory early view of the Falls of St. Anthony. The other proved a bit difficult, for Bradstreet's offering of Father Nicollet near Lake Pepin was rejected as lacking local color. Commissioner Swift hit upon the idea of an early milling scene on the St. Anthony side of the river, and this was duly executed. In the meantime, Bradstreet's contract for the decorating of the council chambers had mushroomed from $1,000 to $2,000, a cost of design by committee.

The last historical interior to draw on the services of an interior decorator was the mayor's office. This time, the Board of Commissioners invited proposals from McIvor, Bradstreet, and a third firm, the Smith and Larson Company. The city's interior designers had learned their lesson by this time: all of the bids came in well above $3,000, or three times the base decorating costs of the much larger council chambers. This apparently was too rich for even the com-

The captain's chairs and leather-upholstered benches created for the mayor's office (at right in 1907) were replicated for the adjoining mayor's reception room designed several years earlier. Scattered pieces of the early furniture, but none of the surrounding decor, survive.

missioners' blood, and the work went to a firm that had submitted a proposal uninvited: Boutell Brothers.

Walter D. and William T. Boutell had begun in business with their father, who set up shop in Minneapolis in 1871. Its primary business from the start had been furniture supply. By the turn of the century, Boutell Brothers claimed to be the largest house, hotel, and club furnisher in the Northwest. The firm had also expanded its line to include all aspects of interior decoration and in the process attracted artisans who could design at a level competitive with McIvor and Bradstreet.

The Boutell Brothers design for the mayor's office was one of the most successful interiors of the Municipal Building. Rather than twisting periods and styles together as Long and Bradstreet had done in the council chambers, Boutell Brothers used the monumental forms and foliate ornament of the Romanesque as a starting point, but brought it up to date by incorporating the simple flowing patterns of the Arts and Crafts movement. The weaving beveled glass pattern of the bookcase doors, elegant scrolled arms of the furniture, and brilliant patterning of the art glass combined to create an air of sumptuousness without pretension.

This John S. Bradstreet landscape—St. Anthony Falls in Early Days—was the first topic settled on for the pair of panels installed in the city council chambers.

The Architectural Arts

Quite apart from the work of those specifically commissioned as designers, the Municipal Building brought late-nineteenth-century architectural arts to a high point in Minneapolis. These arts fused a superb level of craftsmanship with sound manufacturing; all are major components of the building today.

The first of the great building arts to greet visitors today was also the first initiated in the building: the dressing and carving of stone. Each rock-faced block of the monumental granite walling was chiseled to shape and contour on the site. Rather than relying on elaborate carving to relieve the massive surfaces, the architects had some of the blocks sawed and tooled smooth to form belt courses, copings, columns, and capitals. Chiseling, tooling, and sawing were all the work of the granite contractor, James Baxter and Son.

These varied ways of treating stone surfaces created subtler effects than the ornate carving often distinguishing the American or Richardsonian Romanesque style. Elaborate carving never found its way onto the exterior surfaces for several reasons. First was the architects' increasing preference during the design process for monumentality without ostentation. A second factor was the difficulty of finely tooling a rock so hard as granite, particularly when carving in place on a building so massive. The elaborate carving shown in the working drawings of 1888-1889 presumed a building of "freestone," that is, sandstone or limestone, which were comparatively easy to work. Finally, there was the matter of expense. Long and Kees had indicated carving at the middle of each of the corner pavilions, specifically at the springing of the giant arches. The huge, projecting blocks of stone occupying these places still wait for a finish treatment. Similar crude blocks were set in as capitals of the squat columns over the entries, and again at either end of the polished frieze above the Fourth Street entry. Long reiterated the need for finishing this work when the rotunda was formally opened in late 1906, but by that time, the Romanesque style had

The finials of the county-side dormers are carved with an "H" (above), while the column capitals over the Fourth Street entrance (below) still await carving. The Fifth Street tower (right) is a masterpiece of stonecutting.

been on the wane for a decade, and not enough money remained to carry the work through. The architects and builders did succeed in sneaking an extraordinary bit of carving onto the most remote reaches of the exterior walls. Each of the two dormers thrusting from the corner pavilions is crowned with three finials. In a delightful corruption of a rather standard neo-Gothic pattern, the stems of the carved leaves are contorted into an "H" on the county-side finials and an "M" on their city-side mates.

This carving work was the subject of unexpected competition. Local carver and plasterer Henry L. Steinhauser had just formed a partnership with St. Paul carver Joseph Schmid. By offering a lower bid, their firm wedged its way into James Baxter and Son's general contract and got the county-side work in 1892. Two years later, however, when the city-side exterior was approaching completion, William Baxter reasserted himself by bettering Steinhauser's bid, and the major stone contractor for the building got the commission. In both cases, the work was accomplished on the ground, probably in the stoneyard or shop, then brought to the site and hoisted into place. Perhaps the ease of this method was the reason the finials were the only exterior carving accomplished.

The interiors were another matter. When it came time to finish off public spaces inside the building, neither architectural conservatism, material difficulties, nor budget interfered with full expression of the stonecarver's art. This time, the grade of limestone was chosen for its uniformity of texture and susceptibility to rich and delicate carving. Imported from Bedford, Indiana, and often identified by its trade name "Bedford stone," it was locally reported to "have a quality identical with that of the world-famous quarries of Oxfordshire, England."

The areas of the Municipal Building slated to receive most of the Bedford stone surfaces and details were the rotunda and the Fourth Street vestibule, together referred to as the "main entry." When Judge Isaac Atwater wrote his history of Minneapolis in 1893, the entire entry area was to be sheathed in Bedford stone, and Herbert Chalker was to be the primary contractor. Chalker and his brothers and sons (numbering at least seven in all) were a dominating presence in the Minneapolis stonecutting trade during its peak years in the 1880s and early 1890s. Popular tradition linking Chalker's name to the Bedford stonework has reinforced Atwater's account, but both are mistaken. The minutes of the Board of Commissioners as well as contemporary newspaper accounts show that the projected work on the Fourth Street entry was one of the first victims of the cutbacks and delays of the mid-1890s and that the work did not begin in earnest until 1903, three years after Chalker had died. Moreover, by that time, the rotunda had been completely redesigned, restricting Bedford stone to column capitals and other small areas slated for delicate carving. The remainder was to be sheathed in marble.

The springer stones of the Fifth Street corner pavilion arches (above) also await carving, while the Fifth Street entry arch (below) shows a tooled stone belt course. Rock-faced and cut stone alternate in the arcade above the entry (left).

Under considerable pressure from F. B. Long, the Board of Commissioners returned attention to the main entry after the official opening of the city side. This time the main contractor was a Milwaukee firm, Grant Marble Company. A stretch of simple marble carving on the second floor, and quite possibly all of the more elaborate Bedford stonework in the rotunda as well, was therefore executed by anonymous out-of-town craftsmen.

The situation did not sit well with Minneapolis artisans. In March 1906, as the time to finish the Bedford stonework in the main entry approached, local architectural sculptor Herman Schlink put in a personal appearance before the Board of Commissioners to plead the cause of Minneapolis talent. Schlink had already gained local attention for his execution of the plaster filigree for the city council chambers vaulting. He used his time with the board to plead his own cause as well as that of Minneapolis labor in general, providing the Board of Commissioners with an estimate of $5,500.

Schlink was successful in half his plea, for the Bedford stone-carving contract awarded in 1906 went to a local artisan rather than to the Grant Marble Company. The winner, however, was not Schlink but A. A. Gewond, who came in at less than half Schlink's price. Schlink was given fifty dollars for his trouble, but he wrote a letter of complaint, which was duly filed and ignored. Thus A. A. Gewond became the only individual stone-carver whose work can be defi-

A. A. Gewond probably carved these grotesques in the Fourth Street entry.

nitely identified. Some references to the contract confine his work to the vestibule, while others appear to embrace all of the decoratively carved Bedford stonework in the Fourth Street entry, including the humorously grotesque faces flanking the elevators, mistakenly attributed to Herbert Chalker.

Andrew A. Gewond, a native of Galicia (now part of Poland and Ukraine), emigrated to Minneapolis in 1896. Six years later he set up a studio across Hennepin Avenue from the library and began a quiet sculpting business with most of its major clients churches outside of the city. By the time he got the Municipal Building commission, he was a preeminent sculptor, with major commissions for St. Michael's Church in Chicago, the Pillsbury Library in Minneapolis, and a sculpture of Longfellow for the Minneapolis Park Board shortly to follow. Described as "a chubby little man with a face full of animation," he sketched very little in pencil, preferring to move directly to modeling clay, which "minds me better." Gewond had the misfortune to finish his relatively unobtrusive work for the Municipal Building at the same time the *Father of Waters* was installed. So much publicity surrounded the unveiling of the monumental sculpture that the wonderful carvings of Gewond and the Grant Marble Company were overlooked. They were done by artisans equally capable of work in a monumental vein; this just happened to be a humbler commission.

Because it was a major spur to the completion of the city side, the *Father of Waters* played a significant role in the history of the building. This work of sculpture was "discovered" in 1902 by Minneapolitan Roy Herrick while he was visiting the studio of Larkin Goldsmith Mead near Florence, Italy. Convinced it was a perfect symbol of his hometown's dominant place on the upper Mississippi, Herrick immediately set about finding a way to bring it to Minneapolis. In short order, twelve leading Minneapolis citizens and the *Minneapolis Journal* stepped forward to make the purchase and transport it to the city.

The next job was to find a site. Herrick's first choice, a park on the Bridge Square site of the old city hall, failed to materialize, for the city was not willing to demolish the building yet. A letter to the *Minneapolis Journal* on March 24, 1903, urged that the statue be placed indoors and suggested the marble court of the new Municipal Building. In June of the following year Herrick presented the idea to the Board of Commissioners, meeting immediate approval. Once more the donors stepped in to cover the costs of moving the figure to the site, reinforcing the floor beneath, and installing it on a mammoth marble pedestal.

The *Father of Waters* (see page 50) was said to be carved of the largest single block of marble ever taken from the Carrara quarries. As these were the same quarries that the great sculptors of the Florentine Renaissance had used four centuries earlier, Larkin Mead was one up on Michelangelo and his statue of David. Originally named *Mississippi,* the figure symbolically captures the long run of the great river from north to south: pine cones of the northern forests adorn the headdress, a stalk of corn from the farm belt is grasped in the right hand, and an alligator and starfish from the southern delta sit on the base. Soon the sculpture acquired the popular name *Father of Waters,* giving it a meaning specific to Minnesota as well as aligning it artistically with the famed statue *Father Nile,* which it resembled. The only other artwork in the Municipal Building with so strongly topical a flavor was that in the murals and stained glass of the park board rooms.

The spectacular staircase balustrades by Winslow Brothers are of wrought and cast iron finished in black "Bower-Barff" patina.

The second architectural art to reach a high point in the Municipal Building was that of casting and working ornamental metal, magnificently expressed in the ornate iron staircase balustrades of the rotunda, the Fifth Street entry, and the city side on Third Avenue. If the Municipal Building had been begun ten years later, Long and Kees' design for the balustrades would likely have been realized by one of two emerging local giants of the ornamental metalworking industry, Crown Iron and Flour City Ornamental Iron. In the 1890s, these firms could not match the bids of the established leader in the Midwest, Winslow Brothers of Chicago. Crown Iron had to be content with several large contracts for structural ironwork, while Flour City Ornamental Iron split the hodgepodge of lesser ornamental metalwork with Minneapolis Wire Works.

Winslow Brothers was among the nation's leading manufacturers of ornamental ironwork. By 1895, when the Fifth Street entry and county-side stairs were laid, the firm had already completed extensive jobs for the Endicott Building, the Germania Bank Building, and the Pioneer Press Building, among others in St. Paul, and the Boston Block, the Lumber Exchange, the Masonic Temple, and the Public Library, among others in Minneapolis. Each of these commissions demanded ironworking skills of the highest order; the ornate patterns required exact repetition within very narrow tolerances.

The Long and Kees plan called for ornamental ironwork of three quite different types. The lightest of these was open grillwork, in which iron was decoratively wrought and welded or riveted into rigid frames. The original electric elevators ran within cages formed in this fashion; all that survives of them are rough newspaper sketches. Much simpler specimens of this ornamental ironwork once graced several city offices on the second and third floors, also early victims of remodeling. The spectacular staircase balustrades required structural strength as well as open patterning, calling for metalwork of a heavier sort than the open grilles. Wrought and cast iron was the base material of the balustrades, finished in the black "Bower-Barff" patina recently perfected in Chicago. The newel posts were made of bronzed iron, with finials of pure bronze. The architects saved some of their most beautiful Romanesque effects for the third class of metalwork: straight castings molded into low relief patterns. Like the carved granite finials on the highest reaches of the exterior walling, this ornamental work is easily passed by. It occurs in long diagonal stretches at the base of the staircase balustrades emanating from the first floor of the rotunda, and as wide friezes in the second- and third-floor landings of the city-side staircase. Though the heaviest of all the decorative ironwork, its use is purely ornamental; the structure is carried by plain iron strutwork or the walls themselves.

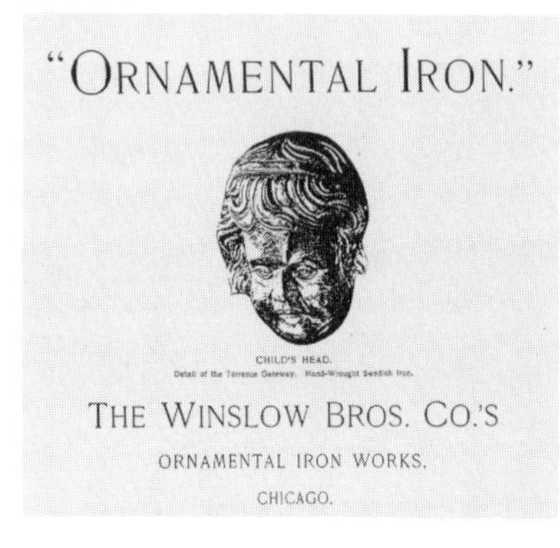

Long and Kees called for another sort of ornamental casting that fell outside the purview of the Winslow Brothers operation. This was the ornamental hardware, visible today primarily in doorknobs and plates (see page 4). All of this was custom-designed by the architects in late 1894, in preparation for the opening of the county side of the building. The practice of architects designing their own hardware was quite new. John Root of Chicago had led the way in the country in 1886. Long and Kees followed Root's lead, specifying designs for the hardware of the Public Library and Lumber Exchange, and E. Townsend Mix followed suit around 1889 in his famed and now much-lamented Northwest Guaranty Loan (Metropolitan) Building. In each case, the architects designed Romanesque swirls of acanthus leaves reproducing in miniature the main decorative motifs of the stone, wood, and plaster carving elsewhere in the building. The Municipal Building designs, with monograms of the city or county woven into the acanthus leaves, were even more elaborate than their predecessors.

W. K. Morrison of Minneapolis won the contract for the hardware, though whether his firm manufactured it is in doubt. The old and reputable locksmith firm Yale and Towne of New Haven, Connecticut, had created a special branch of ornamental hardware around the designs that Root, Louis Sullivan, and other architects had specified, and Long and Kees hardware likely joined these. Like the others, it was available in iron with the black Bower-Barff finish or in bronze. The Board of Commissioners chose the bronze, finished with a dull patina to make it look old.

The light fixtures were at one time among the most ornamental metallic fittings in the building. Nearly all have been replaced over the years. The most regrettable losses were the ornate hanging fixtures in the main courtroom and the city council chambers. Like most of the simpler fixtures, they were of solid brass and designed more for specific decors than for enhancement of the main lines of the building. Their disappearance and replacement was only a matter of time, as interior spaces changed in configurations and function. The monumental iron light standards in the rotunda (see page 50) are another matter altogether. Like the others, they were manufactured in the shops of local supplier Charles Wilkins. They were the most expensive of the options offered by Wilkins and his two competitive bidders, Flour City Ornamental Iron, and Winslow Brothers. Plainly, the Board of Commissioners was not going to be stuck on economic considerations when it came to lighting the *Father of Waters.*

In stark contrast to the artistic airs of Bradstreet and McIvor, Wilkins' business maintained a straightforward, blue-collar profile. His ads and letterhead make the company appear to have been little more than a parts distributor. But the exacting specifications, extreme detail, and exquisite finishes of his light fixtures reveal an operation of quite a different nature. Even after his bid was approved, Wilkins appeared several times before the Board of Commissioners to work out the details of the casting, suggesting that his company had a role in the design as well. The main quibble was about the eagles encircling the light standards just beneath the globe; in Wilkins' initial model, their feathers and ears apparently stuck out too much to suit the commissioners.

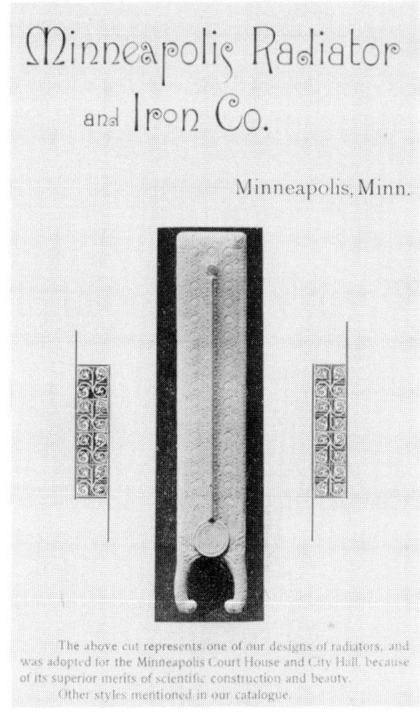

Many winning contractors capitalized on their Municipal Building work in later advertising.

Last but most conspicuous among the building arts coming to fruition in the Municipal Building was that of making stained glass. Art glass designed for specific rooms has long since disappeared, much of it the victim of the 1903 Paulle Showcase fire on Third Avenue. What remains is the showiest glass of all, the five-story wall and skylight of the rotunda. Nothing is known about the individuals who designed the softly toned geometrically patterned windows or the single figurative window centered on the main floor, or even of the initial public response. When the finished rotunda first opened to the public in August 1906, media and public alike were obsessed by the *Father of Waters.* On August 12, the front page of the *Sunday Journal* devoted forty-five inches of print to the statue and the ceremonies surrounding its unveiling, with coverage of the just-finished architectural space that embraced it confined to a single sentence: "The entrance was a noble hall in strength and refinement and a fitting background for the statue."

Despite the silence of the press, the rotunda art glass was an artistic triumph for a local manufacturer as well as an economic coup for the city and county. Serious consideration of local companies had been postponed until the president of the Board of Commissioners could talk to the premier stained glass artist in the country, John La Farge. Apparently a contact with La Farge failed to pan out, for in October 1905, Ford Brothers of Minneapolis was asked to submit samples and designs for consideration.

Concurrently, the Board of Commissioners set up an art glass committee to explore Chicago possibilities. The first Chicago firm investigated was Giannini and Hilgart, which manufactured much of the art glass used by Chicago School architects including the young Frank Lloyd Wright. According to the art glass committee, "they had nothing suitable to show." The Chicago branch of Tiffany Studios in New York was also a washout, for it wanted a minimum of ten dollars per square foot, twice what the board was willing to pay. The committee returned to Minneapolis confident that it could do no better than Ford Brothers.

The committee was not disappointed. In January 1906, Ford Brothers contracted to supply all of the stained glass for the far wall and skylight of the rotunda at the rock-bottom price of five dollars per square foot, and by May the architect reported that "the art glass, which is exceptionally beautiful in color and design, is being made." After a letter from Ford Brothers commenting on the inappropriateness of the remaining plain glass windows, similar stained glass was installed on the side walls of the rotunda.

Until 1896 a glass brokerage firm, Ford Brothers had come out of nowhere to lead the Minneapolis stained-glass industry. The key to its meteoric rise was its employment in 1898 of the great glass artist Robert T. Giles. This had exactly coincided with the loss by its chief competitor, Brown and Haywood, of the brilliant, Tiffany-trained designer W. A. Hazel and the closing of that firm's local design studio in the wake of a merger with Pittsburgh Plate Glass. Brown and Haywood, which had the inside track after supplying all of the beveled glass and Florentine-patterned glass so far, dropped out of the picture.

This Fifth Floor vantage point affords a view into the rotunda as well as of the stained-glass skylight .

Two years before the art glass commission was let for bid, Giles quit Ford Brothers to start up on his own, but by this time the firm's reputation, manufacturing techniques, design staff, and repertoire were established. Giles and Pittsburgh Plate Glass underbid Ford Brothers for the windows on the side walls of the rotunda, but the Board of Commissioners ignored the bidding process and went with the most expensive design by the firm it trusted, just as it had with Charles Wilkins' light fixtures. The production demands on Ford Brothers were so great that the firm drew in an affiliate, Ford Manufacturing Company, which enjoyed an equal reputation in the field of church furnishing.

For all the parties involved in the city hall and county courthouse design, the Municipal Building as completed in 1906 was as free of incongruities as it was rich in detail. This was no mean achievement for a structure almost twenty years in the making. What made it all happen was the continuity of the architectural team at the design board and in the supervisory process. According to contemporary newspaper accounts, the Long and Kees office controlled nearly every aspect of the building's design, from the plumbing fixtures in janitors' closets to the lavish outfitting of public spaces. Even outside suppliers felt the long reach of the architect's hand. The benches in the courtrooms, now placed intermittently along the halls, were manufactured by the Grand Rapids Furniture Company, but they were built according to the design and specifications of Long and Kees. The doorknobs and doorplates were likely manufactured in the East, but Long and Kees supplied the designs and specified the materials.

This bench, originally part of the main courtroom furnishings, now adorns a city-side hall on the second floor.

The Board of Commissioners played an equally important role in ensuring continuity in the design process. Though it occasionally ignored the express wishes of the architects regarding practical or engineering matters, the board continually deferred on matters of design. Even more important, when design choices apparently were left to the commissioners, they quibbled a bit but came down on the side of proposals sensitive to larger aesthetic needs.

Eighty-four years have lapsed since the last "city series" funding was exhausted and the building was nominally finished. Scores of changes have been wrought, many of them greatly affecting the appearance of the interior spaces. It is to the credit of the original architects and builders, the conscientious guardianship of the Municipal Building Commission, and the enduring love of the citizens of Minneapolis and Hennepin County that few changes have been capricious capitulations to changing fashions in design. They have been dictated instead by the changing functions of government, in particular the expansion of services beyond what nineteenth-century planners could have anticipated. Much of the original design fabric of the great public spaces remains, and restoration plans now in hand promise to bring back the splendor of some of the original city-side rooms as well. The Fourth Street entry, long restricted to a single bay, will be fully opened once again. And the clearing of a Fourth Street plaza, urged by F. B. Long as early as 1899, may soon become a reality.

The Municipal Building may never become the secondary hub of commercial development envisioned by its earliest advocates. Instead it stands today as the premier monument of an expanding government services corridor. Over time, the Minneapolis Municipal Building has become the strongest single link in the city and county between the visions and ideals of a nineteenth-century settlement on the plains and the realities of a cosmopolitan urban center today.

Ballot boxes marched past the Father of Waters and up the stairs during preparations for the November 1950 elections.

The Monument at Work

The Municipal Building has provided work and workplace for hundreds of city and county employees and officials from the time its first office opened. This illustrated timeline of its construction, remodeling, public uses, and maintenance might well serve as the basis for a new, centennial time capsule.

July 16, 1891	The cornerstone is laid at a Masonic ceremony with speeches by Mayor Philip B. Winston and Frank F. Davis, a prominent Minneapolis attorney. Within the cornerstone are placed copies of periodicals published in the county and papers related to city and county business and construction.
August 4, 1891	Work stops for the first of several times, due to lack of funds.
February 26, 1893	The state supreme court upholds the county bond issue, reinitiating construction of the Municipal Building.
July 3, 1894	Minneapolis Radiator Company's "improved radiators" with Romanesque design are approved by the Board of Commissioners.
November 16, 1894	The architects give unqualified endorsement of hydraulic elevators but are ignored by the Board of Commissioners.
November 22, 1894	The Board of Commissioners elects to use oak rather than patent steel doors on the county side because of their appearance.

D. & D. Electric Mfg. Company

D·D·D·D·D·D·D D·D·D·D·D·D·D· Minneapolis, Minn.

MANUFACTURERS OF

Dynamos, Motors and Power Generators Electrical Engineers

Contractors for the electric light and power plant in the New Court House and City Hall, Minneapolis, Minn.

D. & D. Electric Manufacturing Company capitalized on its work for the Municipal Building.

March 20, 1895	Bids are opened for Municipal Building furnishings.
April 2, 1895	Brown and Hazen of Minneapolis wins contract to install "Granolithic" sidewalks around the building.
May 29, 1895	The first furnishing bid to escape Minneapolis goes to Gage and Company of Milwaukee for chairs.
July 23, 1895	Local cabinetmaker Roman Alexander wins the first of many contracts for millwork.

The Municipal Building's electric power plant (at left in 1907) had as monumental a presence as the building itself.

July 25, 1895	The contract for cell work in the county jail on the fifth floor is awarded to Pauly Jail Building and Manufacturing Company of St. Louis.
August 28, 1895	The Board of Commissioners overrules architect Fred Kees and decides to install wood rather than concrete floors in the engine room.
September 16, 1895	A storage battery plant is installed to operate the elevators and relieve the dynamos at night.
October 19, 1895	Long and Kees seek bids for willow furniture for the "ladies waiting room."
October 20, 1895	Machinery operating the electrical system in the new building is started.
October 26, 1895	The last piece of granite, weighing three tons, is set in place in the cornice of the northeast turret of the clock tower.
November 9, 1895	Finishing touches are applied to all of the county-side rooms to be opened to the public on November 11.
November 11, 1895	The county side of the building opens to the public amidst great fanfare and celebration; county employees move in a few days later.

This was the largest of the original set of chimes installed in the Municipal Building in 1896.

November 23, 1895	The crow's nest/lookout is put in place 335 feet above the level of the Fourth Street sidewalk.
November 26, 1895	Jacob Fjelde completes the last of his four bronzed busts of judges, which he wants the Board of Commissioners to purchase for the main courtroom.
December 9, 1895	The Board of Commissioners adopts a resolution to have a flagstaff put on the main (clock) tower at the lowest possible cost.
January 8, 1896	The *Minneapolis Journal* reports that a cold snap has caused the recently installed tile in the Fourth Street vestibule to crack and bulge.
February 4, 1896	Attorney Daniel Fish insists that Long and Kees be paid amounts overdue for architectural services.
February 28, 1896	The bells for the clock tower arrive from Troy, New York.

June 2, 1896	John Boland, the architect's representative on the job, resigns as the superintendent of construction.
July 1, 1896	All salaries paid by the Board of Commissioners cease for lack of funds.
August 4, 1896	The construction committee chairman, John De Laittre, resigns from the Board of Commissioners after disagreements over finances and treatment of architects and contractors.
September 8, 1896	Bids are received for a ventilating fan motor for the fifth-floor county jail.
January-April, 1897	Several bills for completing the city side of the building fizzle in the legislature.
March 18, 1898	John Moshik is hanged on a scaffold specially constructed in a vacant area of the county jail, just east of the Fifth Street tower.

John Moshik, the last man hanged in Hennepin County and the only one ever in the Municipal Building, was executed on a scaffold (below) built on the fifth floor.

John C. Grant puts up the first flag for the Municipal Building.

March 18, 1898 — John C. Grant mounts the flagstaff to install the first flag above the Fourth Street tower.

March 20, 1899 — Several Hennepin County legislators say they do not know what the people of Minneapolis want with regard to completion of City Hall.

The Municipal Building Fifth Street side now faces a "water park."

May 8, 1899 — The architects estimate the cost of finishing and furnishing the ground and first floors of the city side at $169,000.

June 21, 1899 — F. B. Long and others recommend the purchase of land surrounding the Municipal Building by the Minneapolis Park Board for a park.

September 22, 1899 — The Board of Commissioners and Hennepin County agree to split the $8,600 cost of a new electric plant for the elevators and lights, as the 1895 system is already antiquated.

October 14, 1899 — Visiting government officials praise the county jail on the fifth floor.

October 26, 1899 — The Board of Commissioners votes not to heat the city side during the harshest months of the winter.

Municipal employees demonstrated a state-of-the-art communications center.

February 6, 1900	Northwestern Mantle Company wins the city-side marble and tile contract and begins design of the city seal for the rotunda floor.
February 23, 1900	F. B. Long reports that the city side will be ready by August 1, underestimating the date by nearly two and one-half years.
May 19, 1900	The clock tower is closed to the public after damage by vandals.
September 8, 1900	The *Minneapolis Journal* reports that the mayor's office will have a private bathtub.
December 4, 1900	The Board of Commissioners ratifies an agreement for the county to furnish heat and light for the city side.
	Mayor-elect Albert A. Ames pressures the Board of Commissioners for occupancy of two floors of the city side.

December 11, 1900	The Minneapolis City Council votes to move into the new building.
December 31, 1900	Estimated cost for finishing the building is $249,000, and Mayor Ames expresses the opinion that all of the work can be done in sixty days.
May 7, 1901	The mayor and police department petition the Board of Commissioners for occupancy of the city side.
June 8, 1901	Work resumes on the city side under a $250,000 "city series" bond issue.
July 11, 1901	The architects submit a redesign of the city council chamber ceiling with a series of Gothic groined vaults.
October 8, 1901	F. B. Long's health fails, and Fred Kees is called to fill in until Long recovers.
April 8, 1902	Grant Marble Company of Milwaukee wins the contract for $140,000 worth of work on the city side and Fourth Street entry
May 6, 1902	Lawrence McIvor and John S. Bradstreet go toe to toe in bidding for decorating of the city council chambers.
May 26, 1902	The Board of Commissioners receives bids for window awnings, called "sun excluders."

"Sun excluders" and flower boxes adorned windows on the Fifth Street side of the Municipal Building about 1906.

June 3, 1902	The Minneapolis Art Commission, formed on April 23, requests city-side quarters.
August 5, 1902	The Minneapolis Art Commission requests and gets its room painted a different color.
November 5, 1902	The Minneapolis firm of Pike and Cook agrees to letter all the office doors on the city side at five cents per letter.
November 21, 1902	Finishing touches are applied to the city council chambers.
November 29, 1902	City aldermen criticize their new chambers for harsh acoustics.
December 15, 1902	The city offices are finally opened.
December 30, 1902	F. B. Long estimates the cost of finishing the building at $321,000.
January 1903	City hall corruption makes headlines such as "Tammany Outdone in Minneapolis" in popular national magazines.

The city council (below in 1905) conducted business amid the visual splendor of its new chambers.

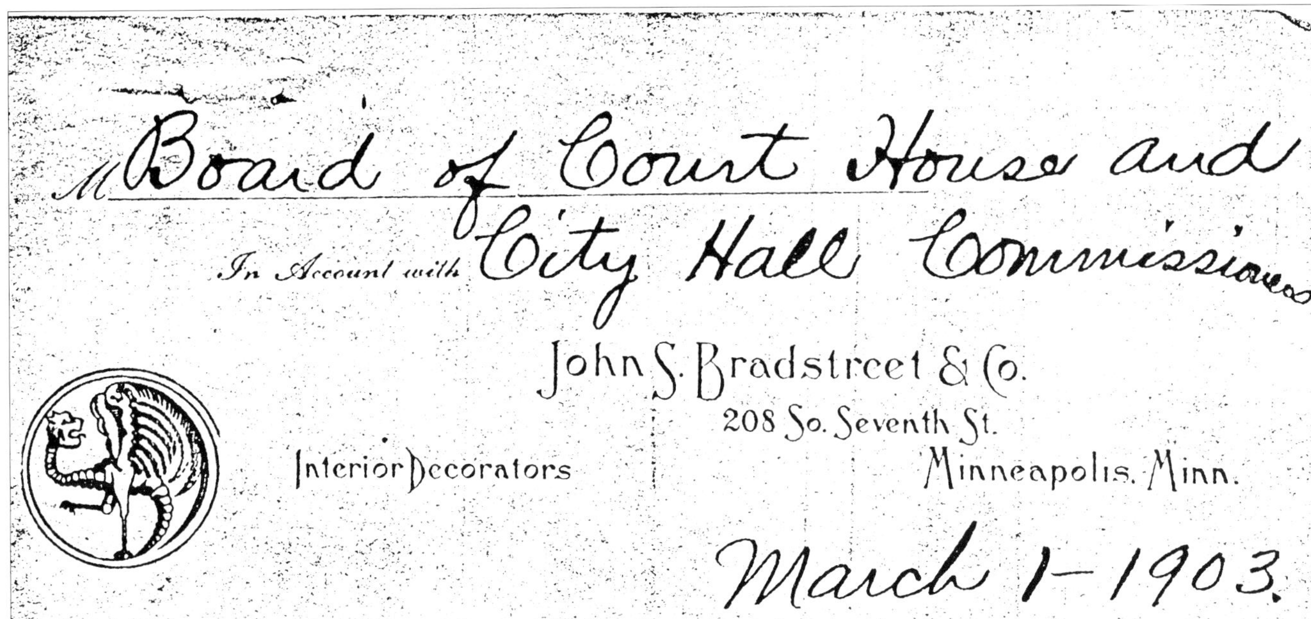
M Board of Court House and City Hall Commissioners

In Account with

John S. Bradstreet & Co.

Interior Decorators

208 So. Seventh St.

Minneapolis, Minn.

March 1-1903.

John S. Bradstreet and Company provided interior decoration for the Municipal Building in 1903.

February 3, 1903	Architect L. S. Buffington requests $100 more in decorating for the art commission room.
March 27, 1903	The teachers' assembly hall formally opens.
April 1, 1903	Plans for a privately financed public plaza opposite the Fifth Street entrance are outlined by William W. Folwell, the first president of the University of Minnesota.
July 7, 1903	The Board of Commissioners votes to cut off light and heat to the city side on August 1 unless the city pays its bills.
July 13, 1903	The drill room disappears from the first floor as the police quarters are expanded.
August 10, 1903	Architects take bids for a bronze historical panel in the rotunda.
	The city council objects to excessive utilities charges and asks for an arbitrator.
September 8, 1903	F. B. Long and Commissioner Edgar Comstock are authorized to inspect jails in San Francisco, Los Angeles, Denver, and other western cities.
November 20, 1903	A heat from a fire in the Leonard Paulle Show Case Factory on Third Avenue breaks $3,200 worth of windows on the city side of the Municipal Building. None of them have been insured because the building is supposed to be fireproof.

The Municipal Building lost a number of windows when the Paulle Show Case Factory, on Third Street (foreground), burned late in 1903.

December 1, 1903	Pauly Jail Building and Manufacturing Company wins the contract for the fifth-floor city jail.
January 4, 1904	The Municipal Building Commission passes a resolution to assume care for the building.
February 4, 1904	A letter from the Municipal Building Commission to the Board of Commissioners demands surrender of the completed portion of the building.

June 7, 1904	The contract with Grant Marble Company is modified to push completion of the rotunda.
June 14, 1904	The Board of Commissioners approves placing the statue *Mississippi* (now known as the *Father of Waters)* in the rotunda of the Municipal Building.
July 14, 1904	The Board of Commissioners formally accepts *Mississippi* from its donors.
November 14, 1904	The main courtroom is declared unsafe after a twenty-pound bracket falls from the ceiling.
January 4, 1905	Thirty-three men apply for janitorial positions in the Municipal Building; eighteen of them are hired.
January 25, 1905	The former civil courtroom is assigned to Associated Charities of Minneapolis.

The Municipal Building was still surrounded by houses when this view from the New York Life Building was made in 1905.

April 13, 1905

The Municipal Building Commission approves the installation of wire screens on the ledges over the Fifth Street entrance, provided they keep the pigeons from roosting there.

April 26, 1905

Mathe Potts asks permission to place a lunch counter in the building.

A representative of the Hennepin County sheriff asks for a sheriff's or jailor's residence in the jail.

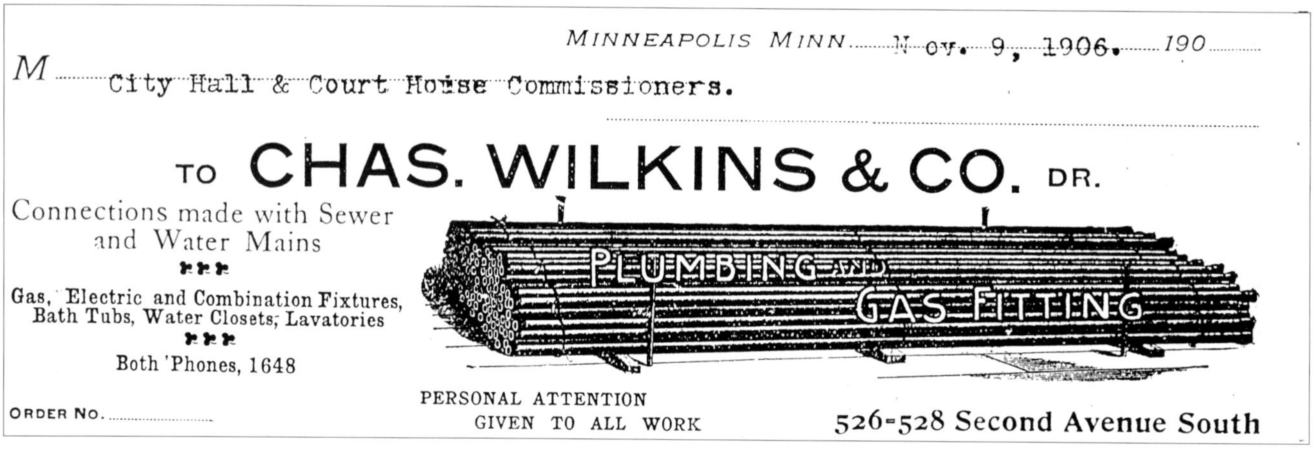

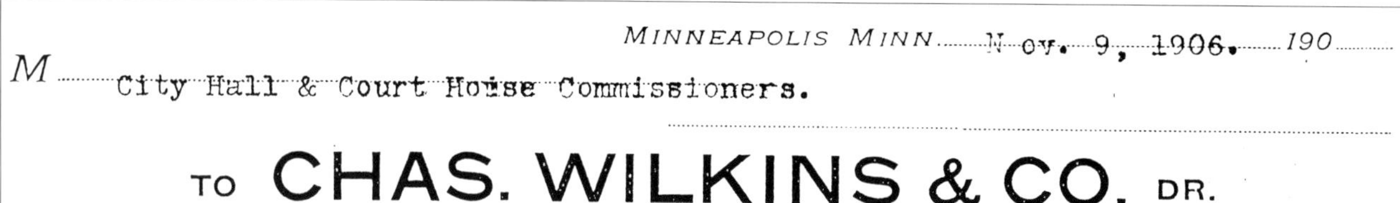
MINNEAPOLIS MINN. Nov. 9, 1906. 190

M City Hall & Court House Commissioners.

TO CHAS. WILKINS & CO. DR.

Connections made with Sewer and Water Mains

Gas, Electric and Combination Fixtures, Bath Tubs, Water Closets, Lavatories

Both 'Phones, 1648

PLUMBING AND GAS FITTING

ORDER NO.

PERSONAL ATTENTION GIVEN TO ALL WORK

526-528 Second Avenue South

Chas. Wilkins & Company supplied the ornate light fixtures for the Municipal Building.

May 16, 1905

Plans for a jailor's flat and a remodeling of the courtyard into an assembly hall and meeting rooms are submitted by the architects.

June 8, 1905

The $37,000 contract to install a marble ceiling in the rotunda is awarded to Grant Marble Company.

June 23, 1905

Losers in the bidding for the decoration of the mayor's office receive $25 each.

July 11, 1905

Minneapolis Street Railway Company receives permission to put bronze eyebolts into the courthouse walls to anchor the streetcar cables.

October 3, 1904

Flour City Ornamental Iron contracts to make a bronze building plaque for installation in the rotunda.

January 2, 1906

Ford Brothers Glass Company contracts to make and install windows of art glass in the rotunda at five dollars per square foot.

February 18, 1906

The Penwell brothers scale the flagstaff of the main tower to make repairs at 400 feet.

February 18, 1906	The *Minneapolis Journal* reports that the MBC saved the city and county $1,000 in fuel during its first year of operation.
April 24, 1906	The Hennepin County Bar Association is notified that its rooms are ready but the association must clean them.
July 24, 1906	Bids are received for bronze doors between the vestibule and rotunda.
August 12, 1906	*Minneapolis Sunday Journal* headlines shout about the "Marble River God Given to the City."
August 24, 1906	The Board of Commissioners decides to rebuild the vestibules to the Fourth Street entrance.
September 25, 1906	The *Minneapolis Journal* reports that the Municipal Building at the anticipated $3.6 million price tag is a bargain that would have cost $6 to $8 million elsewhere.

Horse and carriage traffic is evident in this 1906 view of the Municipal Building from a nearby warehouse.

January 8, 1907	Bids are received for finishing the new art commission room.
February 5, 1907	The Board of Commissioners contracts with Ford Brothers to install art glass in the side windows of the rotunda.
June 4, 1907	The Board of Commissioners accepts the offer of newspaper reporter Albert Dollenmayer to write a historical sketch for its final report.

The Board of Commissioners met in 1907 (above): Clockwise from center foreground are George Brackett, W. G. Nye, architect F. B. Long, (unknown), attorney Daniel Fish, Oliver Erickson (?), secretary L. A. Condit, Edgar Comstock, E. G. Potter (?), Edward Johnson, and Titus Marek.

August 6, 1907	The Board of Commissioners meets at Sweet's Gallery to have pictures taken for the final report.
November 5, 1907	The sum of $516 is withheld from C. F. Haglin's contract until the leaking roof over the assembly hall is repaired.

October 6, 1908	Dollenmayer appears before the Board of Commissioners to apologize for the delay in completion of the final report, which will be contained in a lavishly produced souvenir book.
October 28, 1908	The *Minneapolis Journal* reports that visitors are wearing down the exposed big toe of the *Father of Waters.*
May 18, 1909	The treasurer of the Board of Commissioners reports that the total amount spent on the Municipal Building is $3,557,744.25. The contract for printing the final report is let to Hahn and Harmon for $2,700.00, leaving $3,234.05 in unspent Municipal Building funds.
June 16, 1909	The Board of Court House and City Hall Commissioners performs its final official act, the delivery of property deeds to Hennepin County and the City of Minneapolis.
June 1, 1910	Daniel Fish takes over completion of the souvenir book (final report of the Board of Commissioners), published on October 31, 1910, with 200 copies bound in leather, 500 copies bound in cloth, and 2,500 copies bound in "Old Cloister."

With the transfer of deeds and the printing of its final report, the Board of Court House and City Hall Commissioners (Board of Commissioners) bowed out. Henceforth, the Municipal Building Commission (MBC), established in 1903, became sole caretaker of the building. Under its guidance and authority, the Municipal Building continued to grow and change from within as city and county governments expanded to meet the community's growing need for government services.

November 20, 1909	The Municipal Building Commission authorizes the architects to make plans for installing a jail in the Fourth Street tower.
March 23, 1910	Jail remodeling plans are scrapped because of legal obstacles.
October 19, 1910	The city and county plan expansion of the vaults in the Fourth Street tower of the Municipal Building.

February 26, 1911

A Hennepin County grand jury charges that serious deterioration in the building is due to incompetence fed by political cronyism.

March 1, 1911

The Municipal Building Commission instructs the custodian to see that the nickel-plated plumbing is polished weekly and moves to correct other problems identified in the grand jury report.

Alexander Heine, the city's first airplane manufacturer, circled the clock tower three times as onlookers braved -17 degree temperatures to see the first plane over Minneapolis.

March 2, 1911

The Municipal Building Commission announces plans to install a new ventilating system.

April 8, 1911

Janitors and custodians successfully petition the Municipal Building Commission for double-breasted uniform coats.

April 30, 1911	F. B. Long reports that the original plans for the building are missing.
August 22, 1911	The Municipal Building Commission authorizes the conversion of the humane society office into a courtroom.
August 22, 1912	Municipal Building architect F. B. Long dies at his Minneapolis residence.
January 12, 1913	The first airplane to fly over Minneapolis buzzes the Fourth Street tower of the Municipal Building.
March 17, 1913	A contract is let to build additional rooms for use of the county attorney's office and grand juries.
May 24, 1916	The Municipal Building Commission places on file a petition for a rest room for women employees of the Municipal Building.
March 2, 1919	The Municipal Building Commission assigns several rooms to the Minneapolis Civil Service Commission.

1920	The Board of Park Commissioners vacates its rooms in the Municipal Building.
	The county courtrooms are remodeled.
	Seven homing pigeons, all veterans of World War I, are given a permanent place in one of the towers of the Municipal Building, with provision made for their support for the balance of their lives.
1922	The Municipal Building Commission turns down a request from the city council to use the assembly hall for baseball during the noon hour.
1923	Following the plans of local firm Downs and Eads, a mezzanine is inserted between the third and fourth floors on the city side, dropping the city council chamber ceiling to one-third its original height.
	Joseph Auld and the bell committee purchase three new bells for the Municipal Building chimes.
1924	The Municipal Building Commission investigates the possibility of leasing additional space in a building to be erected across Fourth Avenue at the corner of Fourth Street.
	An assistant county attorney complains of cooking odors from the ground-floor restaurant.
1925	Henry Voegeli, the county treasurer, proposes converting the Municipal Building into a ten-story, flat-roofed skyscraper to take care of municipal needs for the next thirty years.
	Mr. A. Smith complains in a letter that the courthouse chimes play religious music, to which courthouse officials reply that the bells do not have enough accidentals to play "Ukulele Lady."
	The superintendent of Hennepin County General Hospital commends the playing of the chimes of the Municipal Building as a comfort to his patients.
1927	The Civil Service Commission takes up the remaining fifth-floor space in the Municipal Building.
	The custodian removes all candy and nut machines from the building.
1929	The Municipal Building Commission votes to stop leasing space for commercial purposes.
1930s-1940s	The rotunda is taken up during election years by the Voters Registration Bureau and used as a collection area for ballot boxes (see page 72).

Potential buyers and onlookers crowded the rotunda on May 27, 1930, for the auction of the Foshay Tower.

Workers "marched on city hall" in a protest against the Civil Works Administration on April 6, 1934.

1931 New Otis elevators are installed on the Fifth Street side for $34,000.

1932 Joseph Auld's yearly stipend of $100 for playing the chimes is suspended because of the economy and the mayor's irritation at the ringing, but Auld chooses to continue playing them without pay.

1933 The salaries of Municipal Building employees who earn more than $100 a month are reduced by 10 percent because of the depression.

1934 The Minneapolis stonecutters' bid to resurface the Fourth Street entrance under the Civil Works Administration for $23,000 is turned down, accepted, and turned down again.

A demonstration against the Civil Works Administration grows to massive proportion, as thousands of unemployed workers fill the streets around the building.

Part of the tile peak of the Fifth Street tower falls to the pavement, prompting the hiring of a steeplejack to remove the remainder.

1936 New rooms are added to the inner court of the Third Avenue and Fifth Street sides for city assessment records.

A worker brought coal to the furnace from bins under the Fourth Avenue sidewalk (above, in 1939). Girders were raised through the Fourth Street lobby to the second floor to provide space for city assessment records (below, in 1936).

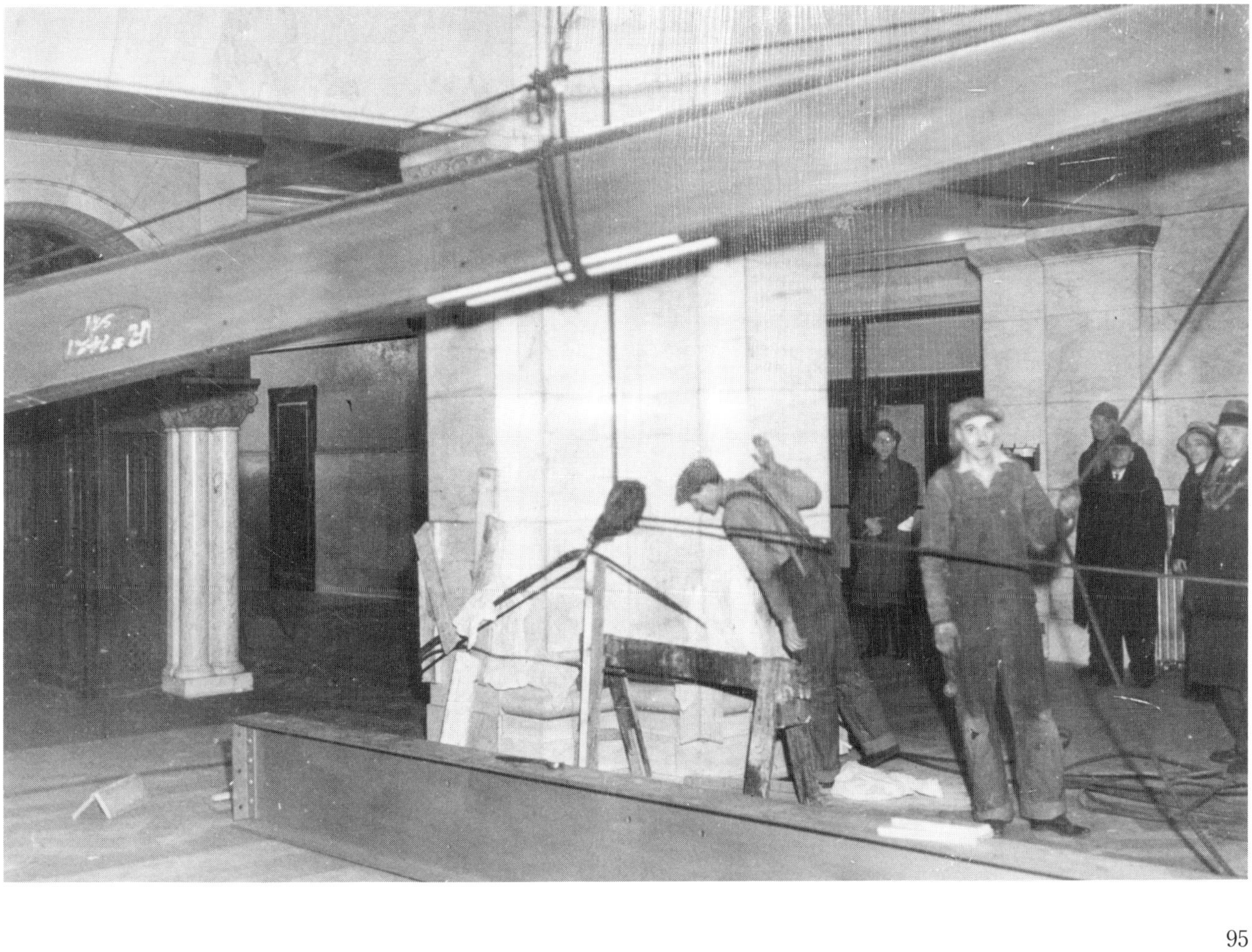

The Father of Waters had his teeth brushed on February 7, 1940, during a cleaning of the rotunda and its furnishings.

Workers cleaned the rotunda stonework on December 15, 1939.

1938	New Otis elevators are installed on the county half of the Fourth Street side.
1939	The city and county consider a thorough cleaning of the exterior, but this is put off.
1939-1940	The *Father of Waters* and the rotunda are cleaned, and the carved Bedford stone is treated with a sealant.
1941	The Minneapolis Aquatennial Association decorates all four entrances of the Municipal Building for the Minneapolis Aquatennial celebration.

Space finished on the fifth floor would provide larger quarters for ever-growing municipal governments.

1942	Structural plans of all floors are prepared as part of a WPA project.
	A complaint is made to the Municipal Building Commission that employees are feeding pigeons roosting on window cells.
1942-1945	The mayor's reception room is used as a Civil Defense office.
1943	To protect against sabotage and theft, lockup hours are established for all entrances.
1945	The Municipal Building Commission calls a pigeon extermination conference for all building operators.

This WPA photograph of the Health Department's chemistry laboratory appeared in the Minneapolis Journal in 1940.

1946	Mayor Hubert Humphrey raises the issue of cleaning the exterior.
	A new elevator is installed in the Fourth Street tower.
	The Municipal Building Commission recommends that the city and county governments consider constructing a jointly operated Public Safety Building.
	Minneapolis City and County Employees Local No. 9 requests approval of an eight-hour, five-day week.

The mayor's office (left, before) was remodeled (below) in 1949.

1947	Downtowners form a committee to deal with the extermination of pigeons.
	Three options for ridding the building of pigeons—poisoning, trapping, and inebriating— are discussed by the Municipal Building Commission.
	Inspection of the plate-glass faces of the tower clock reveals many cracks, and plans for replacement are discussed.
1948	The Board of Education moves out of the building because of crowding.
1949	A set of porcelain steel clockfaces with stainless steel hands is installed in the main tower, and the numerals and hands are outlined with neon tubing.
	Mayor Eric Hoyer's office is stripped of its original furnishings and remodeled to the plans of Long and Thorshov, the third firm in succession from the original architects of the building, Long and Kees.
	A pigeon-elimination program is under way, costing $1,900 during its first year of operation.
1949	The cuspidors in the hallways are transformed into planters.

1949 The *Father of Waters* is dressed as Santa for the holidays.

1950 A copper roof weighing 180,000 pounds is installed in place of the original Spanish tile.

A $500,000 remodeling of the inner court for the County Welfare Department is finished to the plans of Long and Thorshov.

The city-side mezzanine is extended to the plans of architect Samuel C. Wentworth.

1951 The City Building Inspection Department vacates the building.

1952 The fourth floor is remodeled to add courtroom space at a cost of $104,000.

1954 New courtrooms are created in unused space on the fifth floor, facing Fourth Street and Fourth Avenue, for $19,000, and the tower clock is rebuilt by I. T. Verdin Company.

The General Outdoor Advertising Company requests permission to mount a billboard on the roof and is soundly refused.

The Father of Waters entered the holiday spirit in 1949.

This photograph of a "spider cart," invented by Municipal Building roofers to help in hauling and installing copper sheeting, ran in Popular Mechanics in 1950.

1955 Fourth and Fifth Street entrances and three courtrooms are remodeled.

1956 The County Welfare Department is asked to vacate the building because of crowding.

The city council chamber and offices are remodeled for the second time, this time to the plans of Bertil Fasth.

Second-floor county courtrooms are remodeled for $40,000.

1957 The Municipal Building Commission explores the possibility of installing escalators in the rotunda.

Architect Ralph Rapson draws up plans for remodeling the mayor's reception room, but the work is deferred until 1973.

The third-floor courtrooms on the Fifth Street side are remodeled to plans by S. C. Smiley and Associates.

1959 The GAR room is remodeled to plans of S. C. Smiley and Associates.

1959-1960	The Municipal Building is sandblasted and tuckpointed.
1960	Air-conditioning is installed on the ground floor.
1964	S. C. Smiley and Associates draws up a master plan for the Municipal Building.
1970	The Municipal Building Commission adopts a resolution regarding sit-ins and demonstrations and authorizes placement of security screens on lower-floor windows.
1972	Bricks are removed from the back of several stained-glass windows above the rotunda stairs, permitting light to pierce them for the first time in many years.
	The pneumatic bell-chiming system is replaced by an all-electric system, and a fifteenth bell is added.
1973	The Municipal Building Commission rules that the fourth and fifth floors be reserved for the county jail.
1974	The Minneapolis City Council designates the Municipal Building a Heritage Preservation site.
	The boiler operation is abandoned in favor of steam and chilled water supplied by IDS Properties.
	A new jail intake area and a security garage are built to the plans of Ellerbe Associates.
1976	The Fifth Street entry is altered to accommodate a two-story, glassed-in rotunda and a tunnel to the new Government Center, again to the plans of Ellerbe Associates.
	The county jail is expanded on the fifth floor, a new jail built on the fourth, and three third-floor courtrooms remodeled.
1977	A legislative amendment replaces the county auditor and city treasurer spots on the MBC with one appointee from the board of county commissioners and one from the city council.
1978	Emergency Communication moves to the top floor of the interior court.
1981	The City Hall Improvement Review Committee is created.
1983	The Civic Place Plan is formally adopted, assuring revitalization of the building and sensitivity to its historic character.
	The Department of Civil Rights moves into Rooms 239 and 241, the first to be remodeled under Civic Place standards.
1984	The fifth-floor jail undergoes major expansion, for $4.5 million.
	The original wood-frame windows are replaced with anodized aluminum, thermal-pane windows to the level of the third-floor mezzanine for $827,000.

1984 Municipal Building sanitary and storm sewers are separated and new rainleaders are installed for $250,000.

1985 The city side of the ground floor is remodeled under Civic Place standards for the Police Department, License Bureau, and Voter Registration Bureau.

1986 Sixty-six structural beams are modified to meet current building code requirements.

1987 A lower-level sprinkler system is completed.

Confetti clogging the rain gutters after the World Series ticker-tape parade is removed for $2,500.

1989 Eleven thousand square feet of sub-basement is remodeled for the Emergency Communications Center, for $2.8 million.

An emergency generator system is installed for $344,000.

A statue of Hubert H. Humphrey by nationally known sculptor Rodger Brodin is placed in the middle of the Fifth Street side.

1990 A volunteer committee of city and county employees prepares and distributes a 1991 calendar highlighting significant events and photographs of the Municipal Building's first hundred years, announces plans for publication of a centennial book, and begins planning for ceremonies to commemorate the centennial of the laying of the cornerstone.

1991 A $3.1 million electrical and emergency power system upgrade is completed.

Municipal Building Commission 1909-1991

Alexander, Guy W., County Commissioner	1941-1946
Anderson, Barney, County Commissioner	1921
Anderson, William A., Mayor	1931-1933
Andrew, Mark, County Commissioner	1983-1984, 1987
Arneson, Earl, City Comptroller-Treasurer	1976-1977
Bainbridge, A. G., Mayor	1933-1935
Bednarczyk, W. W., City Treasurer	1974-1975
Bloomquist, C. A., City Treasurer	1909-1915 (1913-1914?)
Brown, H. C., City Treasurer	1936-1939
Chase, Henry R., County Commissioner	1916-1920
Cook, Frank W., County Commissioner	1909
DeMars, Louis G., City Council Member	1977-1979
Derus, John E., County Commissioner	1975, 1977, 1978, 1981-1986, 1988-1991
Dickman, Ralph E., County Commissioner	1947-1950
Erickson, Al P., County Auditor	1911-1936 (1913-1914?)
Ferrin, A. R., County Commissioner	1931-1932
Fitzsimmons, Robert F., County Auditor	1947-1967
Fraser, Donald M., Mayor	1980-1991
Hanson, Richard O., County Commissioner	1963-1964, 1976-1977
Haynes, James C. Mayor	1909-1912
Heffelfinger, W. W., County Commissioner	1927-1930, 1935-1938
Hickey, George, County Auditor	1967-1972
Hofstede, Albert J., Mayor	1974-1975, 1978-1979
Hoppe, Vernon T., County Auditor	1973-1975
Hoyer, Eric, Mayor	1951-1957
Hulbert, C. S., City Treasurer	1909-1910
Humphrey, Hubert H., Mayor	1945-1951
Janes, Robert P., County Commissioner	1965-1967
Johnson, Wayne A., County Auditor	1975-1977
Kline, Marvin L., Mayor	1941-1945
Kremer, Richard E., County Commissioner	1979-1980
Kunze, William F., Mayor	1929-1931
Latimer, Thomas E., Mayor	1935-1937
Leach, George L., Mayor	1921-1929, 1937-1941
Makowske, Judy, County Commissioner	1991
Mallon, George H., County Commissioner	1923-1926
Malmquist, Rey C., City Treasurer	1963-1973
Matthews, George W., County Commissioner	1951-1962
Meyers, J. E., Mayor	1919-1921
Miller, Gladys E., City Treasurer	1942-1963
Montgomery, H. A., County Commissioner	1922
Morse, H. A., County Commissioner	1938-1940
Naftalin, Arthur, Mayor	1961-1969
Noot, Arthur F., County Commissioner	1933-1934
Nye, Wallace G., Mayor	1915-1916
Olkon, Nancy, County Commissioner	1979-1982
Olson, Thomas L., County Commissioner	1972-1974

Peterson, P. Kenneth, Mayor	1957-1961
Provo, Jack M., County Commissioner	1969-1972
Rainville, Alice W., City Council Member	1980-1991
Scott, Hugh R., County Auditor	1909-1910
Sivanich, Samuel S., County Commissioner	1977-1978, 1986-1988, 1990
Spartz, Jeff, County Commissioner	1985, 1989
Stenvig, Charles, Mayor	1969-1973, 1976-1977
Ticen, Thomas E., County Commissioner	1975
Upton, R. J., County Commissioner	1911 (1913-1914?)
Van Lear, Thomas, Mayor	1917-1918
Waddell, C. B., County Commissioner	1915
Williams, J. W., County Commissioner	1910

Building Custodians/Superintendents/Managers

Sylvanus Cox, Custodian	1901
William Finke, Custodian	1926
John A. Johnson, Building Superintendent	1947
Dale M. Stanchfield, Superindendent	1952
J. C. Boies, Superintendent	1964
Douglas K. Jacobson, Superintendent	1970
Nancy E. (Noot) Grell, Building Manager	1985

For further reading

The best single source of information about the Municipal Building is still the final report of the Board of Commissioners, entitled *A History of the Municipal Building of the City of Minneapolis and the County of Hennepin, Minnesota.* It was written between 1907 and 1909 and published in 1910. Thirty-two hundred copies were printed; every major public collection in the Twin Cities has one; copies appear now and again in the used book market. The book is illustrated with photographs taken by the Sweet Studio under special commission.

Other early photographs are available for viewing in the Minnesota Historical Society's audio-visual library and the Minneapolis Collection of the Minneapolis Public Library. The latter collection also has a sizable news clipping file on the Municipal Building dating to the mid-1920s.

Preparation of this book and earlier activity by the City Hall Improvement Review Committee spawned several useful compilations of primary material: the Erpestad and Ristuben studies cited in the acknowledgments, blow-ups of newspaper articles published upon the laying of the cornerstone, and an abridged version of the minutes of Board of Commissioners meetings between 1894 and 1910. These are available for study in the offices of the Municipal Building Commission or the Municipal Reference Library in the clock tower.

A Long and Kees office brochure, published in late 1895 or early 1896, provides excellent photographs of most of the firm's major work before 1896, including projects done under earlier partnerships in which Long or Kees were principals. The only extant copies in public collections are in the Minnesota Historical Society Reference Library and the Northwest Architectural Archives of the University of Minnesota. The latter also contains documentation on other work by Long and Kees and information on the two architects' careers.

Architectural drawings of the Municipal Building survive in three places. Several of Long and Kees' measured drawings submitted in the competition (but not the perspective rendering) have been preserved by the Hennepin County Historical Society. Excellent reduced copies of the April 1889 set of working drawings were bound into folios many years ago; at least one complete set survives in the offices of the Municipal Building Commission. Finally, a large number of original ink-on-linen working drawings, most of them dated between 1892 and 1897, are housed at the Northwest Architectural Archives. All of these primary materials are in need of conservation and should be handled with extraordinary care.

In a more general vein, the only book documenting H. H. Richardson's vast influence in this country is the author's compilation of essays, *The Spirit of H. H. Richardson on the Midland Prairies.* As the title indicates, the compilation is restricted to the middle states, but it does provide a wealth of contextual information about the craze for Richardsonian Romanesque buildings in the 1880s and 1890s.

Biographical information about the principals involved in the planning and early operation of the Municipal Building is scattered among various sources. The most important of these are *History of the City of Minneapolis, Minnesota,* by Isaac Atwater and published in 1893 and 1895, and *A Half Century of Minneapolis,* edited by Horace B. Hudson and published in 1908. Both are available in most public collections in the Twin Cities.

Index